Pelican Books
Children and Parents
Everyday Problems of Behaviour

Hermann Peine was Assistant Professor in the Department
of Psychology at Western Michigan University from 1971
to 1974, and is now Psychologist to a community mental
health centre in Utah, working with schools and juvenile
courts.

Roy Howarth is Consultant in Psychological Medicine at
a children's hospital in London, and Medical Director of
an education authority child and family guidance unit.

Children and Parents: Everyday Problems of Behaviour

Hermann A. Peine and Roy Howarth

Penguin Books

Penguin Books Ltd,
Harmondsworth, Middlesex, England
Penguin Books Inc.,
7110 Ambassador Road, Baltimore, Maryland 21207, U.S.A.
Penguin Books Australia Ltd,
Ringwood, Victoria, Australia
Penguin Books Canada Ltd,
41 Steelcase Road West, Markham, Ontario, Canada
Penguin Books (N.Z) Ltd,
182–190 Wairau Road, Auckland 10, New Zealand

First published 1975
Reprinted 1976
Copyright © Hermann A. Peine and Roy Howarth, 1975
Programmes in Appendix 1, copyright © Howard N. Sloane, Jr, 1973

Made and printed in Great Britain by
Richard Clay (The Chaucer Press) Ltd,
Bungay, Suffolk
Set in Times Roman

Contents

Acknowledgements

We are grateful to Dr Howard Sloane, Jr, Professor of Educational Psychology, University of Utah, and Dr Gayle Gregersen, Director, Children's Behavior Therapy Unit, Salt Lake City, for some of the ideas on translating learning theory into practice for the use of parents and teachers.

1. What it's all about

This book was written for ordinary parents, teachers and others who work with children. It is *not* about theories of child development. It is a book about learning, and in particular about the ways in which children learn their ways of behaving, and how parents, teachers and others have an influence on this process. For children not only learn factual knowledge from those around them, they also learn ways of behaving. That is not to say that they only imitate others – what adults do in response to children also has a very important effect on how children continue to behave. This book aims to suggest ways in which parents and teachers, when necessary, can make specific use of their influence to help a child learn ways of behaving which will be both gratifying to himself and acceptable to others.

Underlying the various suggestions made throughout the book is the idea that, whenever children enjoy the reaction of others to the way they have been behaving, it is much more likely that they will act in the same way again for the approval or other sort of attention or reward that they enjoy. In other words, what happens while or after a child does something is one of the most important factors in determining whether and to what extent he will do it again in the future.

Everyone can recall examples of this process in his own family. For instance, when your child is getting on with some activity like drawing, painting, making a model or playing with toys, if you periodically take a look, show your interest or make appreciative comments he is much more likely to persist with his activity and to become engrossed in it on future occasions too. Your interest and appreciation encourages him to behave in that way. Our reactions in different circumstances can have undesirable effects, however. For instance, you may feel that you have to give way to your four-year-old's demands for sweets in the supermarket when he gives a public display of screaming and shouting against your refusal. But buying the sweets in response to his outburst of temper is likely to lead to his learning to do the same again when he wants something you don't want to buy him at the time. Getting the sweets has rewarded his difficult behaviour. So, in order to make use of the suggestions in this book, it is necessary for parents to look carefully not only at the things their children do but also at themselves, so as to understand the importance of their own reactions when dealing with their children.

Of course, the sort of behaviour you decide to teach or encourage in your child – what you define as 'good' or 'bad' behaviour, or 'good' or 'bad' for your child – also depends on you. Some parents are very free in their approach, others more strict. For example, when children are frustrated and angry most parents see the need to acknowledge this feeling and allow it to be expressed in some way; but the degree of tolerance of the expression of anger varies greatly. Some parents will accept any behaviour up to and including hitting out and fighting; others draw the line at verbal abuse, shouting and swearing. Some parents make definite bedtimes for their children; others do not set limits at all. Some parents give explanations for all their decisions and actions and encourage their children to ask questions; others expect children to accept what adults do or say without question. There is a great deal of variation, but the learning principles still apply. What seems to matter most of all, however, is that there is a warm, caring relationship between parent and child.

There is no attempt in this book to deal with serious problems of personality and relationships which sometimes arise in families where there have been major disturbances of family life during the child's early development. Nor is it possible for the methods suggested in the following pages to be used successfully if the parents' emotional relationships with their children have been damaged by unfavourable circumstances or their own childhood experiences. If you are in doubt about the severity of any problem you have with your children, or are concerned about your own emotional relationship with them or other members of your family, you may need the professional help of doctors, psychologists or social workers experienced in this field.

Most people, however, are concerned about the best way to deal with the relatively minor problems of everyday behaviour which we all experience in one form or another. There are times when you may want to turn to books about child development to help you sort out your own philosophy of bringing up children. There are other times when you need to cope with the practical problem of how to deal with your child's behaviour straight away. We all experience this sort of situation: your youngest child who is at home with you all day always demands more attention and gets into a temper when you give the older children tea after school. Or one of the older children gets into the habit of 'showing off', throwing food around and playing messily during the meal. The others all laugh and begin to do the same. Parents don't usually seek advice about such everyday events, but they cause considerable frustration and annoyance. They try one way of dealing with the situation, then another. Grandma makes suggestions, and the neighbours quite different ones. If the parents are not careful they end up by making too great an issue out of what was a fairly simple problem, giving a great deal of attention to troublesome behaviour. When this happens, they often find that it occurs again and again. They begin to think that they cannot win, that they are always going against someone's theory of child rearing; they become frustrated and angry about what they see as their own failure or their child's basic troublesomeness. 'What to do' is what parents want to know; this book aims to provide the general guide-lines so that they can more often answer that question themselves.

Some parents may at first regard much of the approach presented in the following pages as common sense; of course it is, for most people make a happy and successful experience of bringing up their children without ever knowing why. So what we want to do here is to extract and present the main features of the skills which successful parents use as a matter of course, and to suggest ways in which they can be applied systematically by those who have not yet acquired the same degree of self-confidence and skill.

How the chapters are organized

In the next chapter we will look in more detail at the way in which children learn their behaviour, and how we can influence this learning. But first let us describe how all the chapters are organized.

Each chapter is divided into four parts:

1. A quiz: 'What do you do?'
2. Main section
3. Discussion of 'What do you do?'
4. Follow-up quiz

What you will find in the different sections

1. The 'What do you do?' quiz gives you a chance to test your present ideas and ways of dealing with difficult situations. You have a choice of answers to the question – 'What would you do or say in these circumstances?' Imagine yourself in the situation and try to think honestly of what you would usually do.

2. The main part of the chapter contains the information and examples required to make clear the ideas put forward in it.

3. There is brief discussion of the 'What do you do?' questions in the light of the information in the chapter.

4. Finally there is a follow-up quiz to test what you have learned from each chapter before moving on to the next.

Note: The 'Answers' to be found at the foot of the page wherever there is a quiz are suggested answers only. We find that they apply to most children, but each child is different, so your answers may be more appropriate for your family.

2. Learning

What do you do?

What would you do in the following situations? The alternatives are the same for each and are listed at the end of the quiz.

1. Your four-year-old child cries regularly unless you stay with him even when you have read him a bedtime story; he wants you to stay with him and talk. You would like him to settle after a story, without the long ritual each night. Would you do A, B, C, or D?

2. On one of few occasions, your two-year-old plays quietly while you get on with the washing. This is something you want to encourage.
Would you do A, B, C, or D?

3. You are busy with housework and your child brings home a drawing from school. You are pleased but very busy with housework.
Would you do A, B, C, or D?

4. Your child is always coming into the living-room making a noise and doing things to be noticed by adults when you are entertaining your friends, even though he has other children to play with at the time.
Would you do A, B, C, or D?

Answer choices

A   Give him something he likes, such as fruit, praise, a hug or kiss, opportunity to play, etc.

B   Leave him alone and pay him no attention.

C   Scold or threaten him with punishment.

D   Talk to him and explain why he should not do the things he is doing.

There are some things children can already do when they are born; for instance, they cry when hungry or uncomfortable, but most of the things children do have to be learned.

People tend to do things that give them satisfaction, interest, comfort or relief. So events that immediately follow a child's action decide whether that action is more or less likely to occur in the future. If good things follow, there is an increased likelihood of its being repeated by the child, and we say he has *learned* a certain way of behaving. Many

Answers: 1: B; 2: A; 3: A; 4: B+D

things we do every day have been affected by the consequences of our actions on previous occasions. When we open a door, we turn the knob and push or pull, and the consequence of this learned habit is that the door opens. As children, we would just go up to a door and push and bang on it – nothing would happen, and gradually we learned to turn the handle and push or pull. The consequence of this correct action was an open door, and because this was what we wanted, we were more likely to apply the same method when next faced with a door. Very soon there was no hesitation or banging, but the smooth application of the appropriate movements. When an act like this occurs repeatedly it is likely to result in some satisfaction or relief.

A good deal of learning is by example and imitation. Young children learn most of all from what the main people in their lives do. The ways in which they behave are more likely to be imitated if the adult's relationship with the child is satisfying. But even if the relationship is good, learning is dependent on the specific reactions of parents and others to the child's actions. If parents' reactions are not appropriate, children may learn to do things parents would rather they did not do.

Imagine the following situation: Ann is four years old; she used to settle at bedtime without any fuss. Her mother used to kiss her good night, turn out the light, leave the room and that was all there was to it. No problems. One night, however, Ann was scared by a nightmare and cried out Her mother took her downstairs to join the rest of the family watching television. The next night Ann called out for her mother before she fell asleep, and again she was taken downstairs. It soon became apparent that Ann was crying out at night much more than she used to. Eventually her mother decided that she could not come downstairs after she had been put to bed, and told her so; when she left the bedroom this time, Ann began screaming and crying angrily. Her mother, worried that something was wrong, rushed into the room to comfort the child; when she came into the room Ann stopped screaming. From this night on, the mother had to stay with her daughter until she went to sleep; if she tried to leave the room, the little girl began to shout and cry again. Although Ann's mother did not like sitting for an hour or more in the bedroom at night, she felt that this was not as bad as having a scene.

In this situation the behaviour of both mother and daughter has changed. Ann is getting more clinging and her mother is becoming resentful towards her for this behaviour. Let us look closely at how these changes developed.

Most children enjoy the company and attention of their parents. On the first occasion Ann was understandably upset in the night and needed comforting. On the subsequent nights she only required some reassurance, but she got the full attention of her family, and in particular of her mother. She began to learn that crying out at night brought this attention and, although she did not deliberately decide to cry or scream, this became her regular night-time behaviour. When her mother tried to put a stop to it, the crying turned to screaming and an angry tantrum; and her mother gave in. It began to look as though Ann was in control. She had learned this behaviour to get what she wanted – joining her parents downstairs. Ann's mother was giving in to her daughter because this avoided a scene, which was something she did not know how to handle. In a sense this mother was getting some relief herself for staying with her child at night, because no tantrums occurred if she gave in. But she had to pay the price!

You might call this an example of a vicious cycle. It can be illustrated like this:

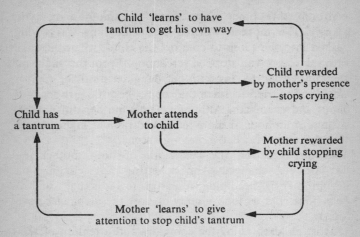

The next example shows how parents can take more control over the consequences of a child's behaviour to influence what he does.

In John's family learning was also taking place, but this time it was learning which everyone in the family was pleased about. John had not been doing very well at school. One day he brought home a drawing. His mother showed how pleased she was, giving him a big hug and praising the picture. John started to bring things home from school more often, for each time the whole family showed how pleased they were. Of course, his parents give him the most attention for his good work, and John has begun to bring home only his best work. He is also trying harder to do as well as he can at school. John has learned that in his family it is worthwhile to do well at school; when he does good work at school, good things happen at home. Soon he will want to work for his own sense of achievement. Both Ann and John were clearly affected by the experience that followed what they did.

16

Parents can influence their children's behaviour by rewarding them in some way after they have done things they want to encourage. However, it is not always easy to appreciate what an individual child finds rewarding. At times we can only judge what is gratifying to a child or an adult by observing the usual consequences of his actions: the things that give some children satisfaction do not do so for others. Parents often think of rewarding their child with sweets, toys

and other objects or activities that they know they like. Attention, however – interest, care or praise – is often more important. Attention can be so important, in fact, that even in the form of scolding or punishment it may still be satisfying, especially if the parent does not give attention for 'good' behaviour at other times.

For example, Peter was a lively, adventurous boy who for four years had been the only child and also the first grandchild of the family, and consequently received a good deal of attention. When his sister was born he inevitably got less attention from his parents and grandparents, and during the next few months began to be very difficult. His parents were driven from quiet reasoning with him to scolding, and finally to smacking, for some of his provocative 'showing-off' and tempers. However, his troublesome behaviour seemed to increase with each punishment rather than get better. It became apparent that Peter was obtaining the attention he had formerly been accustomed to by provoking punishment from his parents, and that even smacking was satisfying in this respect. Many teachers are aware that children are naughty simply to get their attention. In some classrooms children can get more than three quarters of the teacher's attention by being troublesome. As parents do at home, teachers tend to give a good deal of attention to children by irritated reactions when they are being difficult, but have a tendency not to notice or just feel relieved when they are being quiet and 'good'.

Knowledge of the way in which people learn indicates that we should try to reverse these responses towards our children's behaviour. This means taking notice and sometimes praising when your children are doing things you want to encourage, while at other times paying no attention to their more irritating behaviour. Sometimes it is obviously not possible to ignore destructive or aggressive acts, but ways of dealing with these without making them more likely to recur are discussed in a later chapter.

Discussion of 'What do you do?'

It is the way in which we react to a child's actions which determines whether he will continue to behave in that way. So let us now see whether answers A, B, C or D would encourage or discourage a child from behaving in the ways described at the beginning of the chapter.

A Giving a child something he likes increases the likelihood of what he has just done occurring again or more frequently.

B If a child's behaviour is intended mainly to get your attention and you ignore it, he will slowly learn to give it up and try something else instead. (Perhaps you should be thinking of ways to give him attention at other times when he is 'good'.)

C Scolding, etc. can be satisfying in itself, and even if it does act as a punishment, the effect is usually only short-lived. (See Chapter 6, p. 67.)

D For most children explaining the 'rules' helps, but this alone is usually not enough, especially with younger children. Your expectations about their behaviour should

19

Children and parents

always be stated in advance; if you give the 'rules' after some unwanted behaviour has occurred, then you are again giving attention for something you wish to discourage.

Fuller answers to 'What do you do?'

1. If your child is crying only to keep you with him longer at night, the most effective way to get him to settle is to leave him quietly, without fuss, after saying good night (B). This may be very difficult at first; you may even not be able to do it without help, but sooner or later, whatever else you try, you are likely to have to take this step.

2. Even though you are busy, it is worth while breaking off briefly to give some indication that you have noticed his quiet independent play (A).

3. Attention and praise for the drawing will encourage your child to bring more school work to show you, and may stimulate his interest in subjects at school (A).

4. Ignoring this not very troublesome but irritating behaviour is the most effective way to bring it to an end (B). Unfortunately, your visitors may give the attention instead. With older children explanations (D) before the next visitors come may help them to learn not to interrupt.

Follow-up quiz

Fill in the blanks with the most appropriate of the following words:

20

A satisfy (ing)
B ignore (d)
C punish (ed)
D explain (ed)
E encourage (d)
F vicious cycle

John, a big three-year-old, used to scream whenever he didn't get his way, and his mother often shouted at him when he got into these tempers.

His mother shouted to (1) .... John for his screaming. In effect, her shouting did not (2) .... but rather (3) .... his screaming. We know it was (4) .... because John's screaming continued. It would have been better for John's mother to (5) .... his screaming rather than (6) .... with attention. Trying to (7) .... to John what he was doing was very difficult at his age, and again this would have been giving him extra attention at the time he was screaming which is (8) .... and maintains John's outbursts of temper. The situation is a (9) .... with Mother's scolding giving John attention and causing him to be quiet (but not for long). John's mother's reward is the brief rest she gets between battles.

If you were unable to answer all the questions, look again at the discussion section.

Answers: 1: C; 2: E; 3: E; 4: A; 5: B; 6: E; 7: D; 8: A; 9: F

3. How and when to use rewards

What do you do?

Choose one or more of actions A, B, C and D for the following situations:

1. Your one-year-old child says 'Mama' for the first time as you put him in his cot; you are pleased and you want to encourage him. Would you:
   A Get his feeding bottle ready and give him a drink from it as a treat, as he rarely uses it now.
   B Say 'Mama' back to him.
   C Play with him in his cot later in the morning.
   D Smile, pick him up and give him a hug.

2. Your ten-year-old child has brought home a good school report. Would you:
   A Give him something that he likes to eat.
   B Praise him.
   C Say that as a reward he can stay up late that night to watch television.
   D Praise him and say that because he has done well you will put money in an account for use later in his school career.

3. You are encouraging your twelve-year-old child to polish his shoes regularly as part of a number of chores he helps with. Whenever he remembers to do this would you:

A Say 'How nice your shoes are looking', or make a similar comment.

B Give a small treat.

C Take him to a film or other entertainment that evening.

D At the end of the day, say how well he has done his chores that day.

4. Your four-year-old is trying to tie shoe laces. Would you encourage him with praise:

A At each attempt.

B Once a week for trying.

C At the end of the day when he goes to bed.

D When he finally achieves a perfect bow.

In the last chapter we said that whatever happens while or after a person does something influences how that person behaves on future occasions. Whatever the person is doing, if what happens as a result or in response is pleasing or satisfying to him he is likely to behave in the same way more often or more strongly. We can say that this particular way of behaving has been encouraged or *reinforced*. It is reinforcement that keeps a child doing everything he has learned, whether it is regarded as 'good' or 'bad' behaviour. Anything that a person finds rewarding will reinforce the way he behaves. For children the rewarding things may be tangible rewards, such as toys, comics, books, play materials, drawing, painting or craft equipment, items to go with an established collection (like foreign stamps) or to start a new collection, sweets, money, marks, points, stars or other tokens.

Other rewards which will reinforce children's behaviour

Answers: 1: B, D; 2: B, C, D; 3: D; 4: A

are activities. These may range from fairly passive experiences like watching television, listening to stories, looking at or reading books together, to being given a chance to let off steam without restrictions for a while, staying out later in the evening, or staying up later at night. Activities are often most rewarding if they involve the participation of a parent with young children or of friends with older children: for example, building complicated models, playing board games, going on a fishing or walking outing, arranging a party or dance. By their nature these kinds of activity can usually only be deferred rewards, taking place some time after the behaviour you wish to encourage or reinforce. However, the initial and immediate reward can be the promise (followed by the giving) of help from parents or other adults in arranging, setting up, or getting started something that the child would find difficult to do alone.

The rewards for children which can be most readily and immediately given, and are often the most important and successful, are the various forms of attention from parents and others, such as interest, affection, praise, approval, support, agreement and congratulations. These may be shown by actions such as a smile, hug, kiss, a pat on the back, an arm round the shoulder, or by words such as: That's good! Right! Well done! That's just what I think. That looks (or sounds) interesting. Beautiful! Fantastic! I like that.

There are two further general points to consider when you are thinking about how to reward children's behaviour:

1. A particular reward may not be satisfying to all children, and may not satisfy the same child at all times.

2. Simple attention from adults, being a powerful reward, will almost always influence children's behaviour and should therefore be given in preference to other kinds of reward or in combination with them.

Encouragement or bribery?

Many parents, when thinking for the first time about the deliberate and conscious use of rewards, become concerned about whether what it all amounts to is really bribery or blackmail, and therefore undesirable.

In blackmail unpleasant events are threatened unless certain actions are carried out. There are, however, no threats of punishment or anything else in the method advocated here. In bribery, pleasant consequences are promised if certain actions are carried out. The original meaning of the word implied that the activities being induced by bribery were illegal or unethical and usually only of advantage to the briber. If there is any doubt about whether what you are encouraging your child to do is infringing his rights as a child, or is dishonest, then you clearly should not even be considering making promises of rewards. We hope that what you will be trying to encourage in your child is behaviour which will be helpful to him in his social development and an advantage mainly to him, though it may bring secondary satisfaction to yourself and others.

For young children, in any case, the promise of 'rewards' of any sort in the future is rarely successful in getting them to behave in some specific way. What we have stressed is the need to give an encouraging reaction during and immediately after behaviour you like in your child. This is obviously more difficult for many parents who have got used to trying to change their child's ways by dangling in front of him future big rewards (bicycles, radios, etc.) in return for his co-operation now. Any effect gained in this way tends to be short-lived.

Contracts between parents and their older children (as discussed in Chapter 8) may be seen as near to bribery. But the true briber, though seeming to have an advantage, is always vulnerable, because the value of the bribe has to be raised again and again as a result of his 'victim's' further demands. Therefore, when contracts about behaviour (such as time in at night, or amount of help given in the house) are being agreed between older children and their parents, there should be no advantage taken by one side or the other. It must be a true contract with both sides offering something in return for what each would like out of the contract. This allows a basis for sensible compromise – both sides are free not to enter into the contract or to withdraw, and have the full knowledge that if the agreement is not fulfilled by one side, then there is no need for the other to do so either. This is not bribery; there are positive elements to the arrangement which help the older child to learn about fair and honest social interactions.

Timing of rewards

It is not only the kind of reinforcement that is important, but also when it is used. In giving a reward to a young child it is very important to give it while or immediately after he does something you want him to learn or develop as a habit. If you delay the reward you may find that you have by mistake encouraged something he does later.

For example, a mother wanted her seven-year-old daughter to learn to clean her teeth each morning. She decided that she would give the child a reward in the form of an inexpensive but colourful foreign stamp to go in her collection whenever it was not necessary to remind her to brush her teeth. The mother started by giving the stamp just as her little girl was leaving for school, about half an hour after she had brushed her teeth and when she had done various other things in the meantime. The girl's mother was disappointed to find that her daughter still frequently forgot to clean her teeth in the following weeks. She also noticed that the little girl was beginning to put her coat on and leave for school earlier than she used to. The occasional reward of the stamp was having an effect on the child dressing and leaving for school because it was given close to the time that happened, and failing to have its desired effect on the teeth-cleaning, which occurred half an hour earlier when it occurred at all. When the mother eventually gave the stamps *immediately after* her daughter cleaned her teeth she found she brushed them regularly, and it became an established habit which later did not depend on the reward of a stamp; the feeling and appearance of her cleaned teeth were rewarding in themselves.

So when you are trying to reinforce some way of behaving in a young child it is important that the reward should follow *immediately after or during* the child's action, rather than after a lapse of time. It is also necessary at first to reward frequently in response to even the smallest sign of the behaviour you wish to encourage.

It soon becomes apparent, however, that you can't spend all your time rewarding your children each time they do something you like. The everyday activities of parents simply don't give time for this. What happens when different ways of encouraging children are used? For example, what happens when a child is given attention *each* time he behaves in a certain way, as compared with only once in a while? We have already seen that when a child is encouraged each time he does something, he tends to do it more frequently. He also begins to expect to receive some attention for doing it. Under these circumstances, learning is very rapid; the method is, therefore, useful in encouraging the initial development of a particular habit or teaching a new way of behaving. But what happens once we stop the encouragement, attention or rewards? The child quickly learns that he can no longer expect this sort of reward and his newly acquired habit equally quickly disappears.

This happens with most of us. For example, if a chocolate or cigarette machine which has previously been reliable fails to deliver the goods when we put our money in, we may kick the machine, swear and rattle the handle about vigorously, but most of us would be very hesitant to put in further money. If we do and again the machine fails, it is unlikely that we will continue to use it. The behaviour – 'money in the machine' to receive 'goods out of the machine' – has quickly petered out. So the important thing to remember is that in circumstances where rewards are given *each time* a child does something learning takes place very rapidly, but that this process is also rapidly reversed when the rewards are stopped.

In ordinary family life, especially with older children, it is not necessary to give attention or some other reward each time the child does something you wish to encourage. Instead, encouragement may be given only after several instances of the particular behaviour (perhaps every three or four or more) and at varying intervals. The child then never knows when the reward will be given. This is how most parents usually reward their older children. When the rewards are eventually given less often, the children still continue to do what their parents want, and they may also be starting to see why that behaviour is thought to be most useful and sensible. For example, you may want an older child to keep up his table manners even when he is not at home. It is clearly not always possible to remind him. This is one of the circumstances, however, when commenting on his good table manners every now and again suffices.

In fact, many older children's and adults' activities depend on and are kept going by this type of intermittent encouragement from others. We do not need a reward every time we do something. We now understand why certain behaviour is desirable and we may get satisfaction from many activities but, still, some sort of encouragement for our various actions occurring every so often maintains our 'good habits'.

Let's recapitulate what has been learned in this chapter.

Increasing the frequency or strength of a certain pattern of behaviour by giving rewards, praise or attention after it has taken place, we have started to call *reinforcement*.

The following facts have been learned about reinforcement:

1. What is reinforcing for one child's activities may not be so for those of another child, but some praise and attention from adults tends to be generally useful in reinforcing children's behaviour.

2. In encouraging young children to use particular aspects of their repertoire of behaviour it is necessary to reinforce the particular activity immediately after its occurrence, and to do this frequently.

3. For children of most ages, reinforcement after each performance of a particular activity is the most efficient method when first starting to encourage that activity. Later, once the habit is established, occasional reinforcement is all that is needed to maintain it; or it may maintain itself because it is now in itself rewarding to the child.

Discussion of 'What do you do?' (p. 22)

1. Attention from the mother or food would probably be a reward for most infants, and so reinforce their actions. Remember, however, that it is the time between the child's action and when the reward is given which is

important, so that a combination of (B) and (D) would be best.

Getting a bottle ready (A) is too long delayed to be an effective reinforcement. The long time-interval before playing with the child (C) would make it act as a reward for other actions later in the morning.

2. Different children vary greatly in the way they react to different rewards, but most ten-year-olds would probably not find something to eat (A) a sufficient reinforcement to encourage further work at school. Praise (B) can be given immediately and is very effective. Whatever else you do, you will want to praise as well.

The delay of a few hours is usually too long for a reward to be effective for a ten-year-old; but, coupled with praise, the extra television time (C) would probably be very effective. Giving money alone (D) would not be effective for the same reasons as (A); but paired with praise you might also be teaching him something about saving.

3. When first encouraging a child to do something like shoe cleaning, a treat (B) or praise each time (A) will be most effective in getting him started. A film (C) is too long delayed and too big a reward. Congratulations later in the day (D) is the sort of reward that is needed later to keep the habit going.

4. Training a young child to tie his shoe laces requires at first a reward each time an attempt is made to improve (A). Rewarding at the end of the week (B) is too long a delay, as is the end of the day (C), which is also when he is about to shed his shoes and go to bed – the opposite of tying the laces. If you wait until your child finally manages to complete a task of this sort perfectly (D), you

and he may be waiting a very long time if you do not give him any encouragement earlier on. Praise is a very satisfying reward which parents are able to give freely and readily.

Follow-up quiz

Answer the following:

1. When children are learning something new, reward them
   A at the end of the day
   B when they do the new task
   C every now and then

2. When children have learned a habit, such as putting their clothes away, it is a good idea for parents to
   A never reward this piece of behaviour
   B reward every so often without the children knowing when
   C reward on the same day each week
   D always give a reward when it occurs

3. Susan washed up the breakfast dishes at 8.00 a.m.; tidied her room at 8.30 a.m.; had a fight with her brother at 8.40 a.m. At 8.45 a.m. her mother had noticed that Susan had washed up and tidied her room and praised her in general terms for being a good girl. Which of Susan's actions that morning was most probably influenced by her mother's general praise?
   A washing dishes
   B cleaning room
   C fighting brother

Answers: 1: B; 2: B; 3: C. If you were unable to answer all the questions, look again at the discussion section.

4. Describing children's behaviour

What do you do?

Would you describe the following accounts of behaviour as clear or not clear? Indicate by writing C (Clear) or NC (Not Clear) in the space in front of each sentence.

.... 1. John was out of his seat six times between two o'clock and two-thirty.

.... 2. Billy was naughty twice today.

.... 3. Jean is playing happily in the garden.

.... 4. Peter behaved well at the dinner-table today.

.... 5. Alan cried every time his mother left the nursery school-room.

.... 6. Kathy has a tantrum every day on the school bus.

For two chapters now we have been considering how children learn their everyday behaviour, and we have shown that the events which immediately follow a child's actions are of utmost importance in determining his future actions. This point is so important that we have stated it over and over

Answers: 1: C; 2: NC; 3: NC; 4: NC; 5: C; 6: NC

again. Once a parent realizes that the type and timing of his own reactions to his child's behaviour is crucial, then he is in a position to get on with helping his son or daughter to develop appropriate ways of behaving.

The first task in trying to make these changes is to decide and describe precisely what your child does that you would like to change. This may sound simple, but in fact it is

Jane was naughty today

difficult. It is, however, very important in carrying out the procedures described in this book. Don't be put off – exercising your powers of observation as shown in this chapter will soon enable you to define and describe your children's activities clearly.

We can speak of children being 'naughty' or doing something 'bad', but what do different people understand by these phrases? Obviously it is impossible to know what has happened – whether the child has really been 'difficult' or whether the adult concerned has been more than usually critical. What one parent regards as undesirable behaviour, may be seen by others as only an occasional lapse in the development of more mature behaviour.

Imagine that Billy has just been sent away from the dinner table for refusing to eat peas and flicking them at his sister. He stamps off to his bedroom and has a violent 'tantrum'. In recounting this episode you might just say that he had been 'naughty'. But several aspects of this situation remain unclear. We know what he did that made his parents ask him to leave the table – but can we all agree what a 'tantrum' is? Just what did he do in his room? How long did it last? When did it start and stop? If you had said that when Billy got to his room he threw his toys about, kicked furniture and the door and screamed for five minutes, we would now have a better understanding of what actually happened. Again, if a teacher says that Matthew behaved very aggressively in the playground today, just consider all the possible interpretations of this statement that might have been made.

This lack of precision in the use of language leads to a number of problems. We will now look briefly at three of these, all interrelated.

First, people tend to *interpret* behaviour rather than *describing* what has happened. The word 'aggression', for instance, may mean one thing to one person, and something entirely different to another. You have all experienced this sort of problem, especially in trying to explain to people who are also looking after your children, such as teachers or doctors, just what has been happening that you want to tell them about or wish their advice on. You think you are being clear, but discover afterwards that the other person has not understood the problem and is having to try to clarify it for himself with questions. This may lead to irritation on both sides and hinder your obtaining the help you are seeking. It often happens because the words used are *interpretations* of what has been going on, rather than straight *descriptions*. For example, people's actions are described as 'nice' or 'nasty', 'aggressive' or 'submissive', 'good' or 'bad', etc. rather than by what they actually consist of.

Secondly, vagueness in description interferes with any sort of measurement or assessment of a child's activities. When parents describe an event imprecisely, how can they know for later comparison how often or how long it occurred, or even when it occurred? Teachers in school want to know whether their teaching methods are increasing their pupils' understanding. They do not assume that the pupils are steadily increasing their knowledge, but check the change since the last piece of work or test results. Similarly, parents who wish their child to give up some long-established habits and to learn different forms of behaviour need to know clearly if a real change has taken place rather than rely on wishful thinking.

Third, the possibility of altering a child's behaviour is hindered by poor definition and description. If the description of a child's activities is vague, it is very difficult to be sure of exactly what you are trying to change, and how to set about it. If you do not know clearly what to reinforce, your own behaviour is likely to be inconsistent, learning will be slow and children will sometimes learn things you do not want to encourage. Tidiness is the sort of thing you need to define for both your child and yourself if you want to help him be more orderly.

Here is an example: Martin had become exceptionally untidy, to such an extent that he could never find anything he wanted in his room; everything was all over the place. His mother wanted to help him become at least tidy enough not to lose things all the time. Before she could set out to do this she had to be clear what she meant by 'being tidy', so that she knew exactly what to reward Martin for. To begin with, as he was only seven, she decided that if he put away the toys he had played with that day, it was enough to get a reward. As he grew older her definition of 'being tidy' changed, so that when he was ten she also expected his clothes to be put away and that he should make his own bed. A year or two later Martin had learned that having an orderly room is rewarding in itself, and at this stage he began to set his own standards.

Now let us look at some more examples of the three problem areas in giving clear descriptions.

If you manage to describe an aspect of your child's behaviour in such a way that it means the same to most people you describe it to, you will have largely passed this first test of being able to observe and describe clearly what he does. An infant-class teacher could describe the arrival of a new five-year-old at school over her first three days in the following way. On the first day she cried and would not take her coat off for five minutes, then settled into class activities with enjoyment; on the second day she sobbed for about half a minute and looked after her mother out of the window before settling into class activities; on the third day she did not cry, waved to her mother at the door and came straight to her table to find her work-box. From this description we know a good deal about this little girl settling into school; ambiguous words and terms have been avoided, and just what the child did has been described. Her mother, however, might well have described the same events to a neighbour thus: 'She was very upset when she first went to school, but settled down after a while.' The phrases about what the little girl did – 'very upset' and 'settled down' – as well as the phrases about timing – 'when she first went' and 'after a while' – are all unclear. One might think from the mother's description that the little girl's reaction to starting school was anything from a severe emotional disturbance to the ordinary initial reluctance to separate from mother.

Another thing to remember is that your judgements about behaviour tend to change, not only as time goes by but also from one situation to another, so that it is important for clarity's sake to avoid judgements and describe just what happens. For example, a parent regarded spilling food on the table while eating as bad-mannered, but only really noticed this when his child did it while visiting other people. He might say then that Simon behaved badly during tea with his uncle today. On the next day at home when the same thing happened he might notice only that no squabbles occurred between Simon and his sister, and therefore comment that Simon behaved well at table today. If this father had described in detail what Simon did on the two occasions, he would have seen that the same behaviour occurred in each situation, and that it was his own recognition of it that varied from place to place. Alternatively, suppose that Simon's father's attitude to table manners changed over a period of a few months, so that whereas he used to regard spilling food on the table as bad manners, he later believed that this sort of thing did not matter. Then to say on one occasion that Simon behaved badly at tea (because he spilled food), and at a later time to say how well Simon had behaved at tea (although Simon had again spilled food on the table) is to make confusing statements, sounding as though the child's behaviour had changed, whereas in fact it was the father's attitude that had changed. This point needs to be stressed – parents should always check on their own behaviour to make sure they are being consistent. They may quite often find that it is inconsistency in their own behaviour towards their child that causes problems.

Children and parents

The following descriptions are examples of clear and unclear definitions of what children do.

Clear	Unclear
Johnny hit three different children with his fist at playtime this morning.	Johnny has been aggressive today.
Sue spilled her milk once during teatime on both Tuesday and Friday.	Sue is a messy eater.
Bill played with building bricks for half an hour with his sister this morning.	Bill was a good boy this morning.
Marion brushes her teeth every morning and night.	Marion knows how to brush her teeth.
Anthony doesn't sit in a chair for more than one minute while listening to a story.	Anthony is over-active.

Does this kind of accurate observation sound as though it would make parents become too detached? This is an objection often made. However, parents who take a little time and trouble to make accurate observations and clear descriptions of both their actions and those of their children find that this not only ensures that they are able to make use of knowledge about their interaction with their children, but also improves their understanding of and relationship with each child. This is surely the only way to be fair. The next chapter deals with recording and graphing information on what children do, and will give you additional help in clarifying and taking some of the guesswork out of changing their ways of behaving.

To conclude: if you do not define clearly the aspects of your child's behaviour that concern you, difficulties arise in (1) communication of the problem to others, (2) assessing the severity of the problem, and consequently (3) the possibility of altering his way of behaving.

These difficulties are, of course, all related. In order to overcome them, you should limit yourselves to descriptions of behaviour in terms of observable events, that is, what the child does in a certain situation. When you have observed your child's actions and have described them clearly, you should be able to answer 'yes' to the following questions:

1. From the description alone, would any two people agree as to what the child is actually doing?

2. From the description alone, is it clear when and how the particular activity begins and ends?

3. Is the description clear enough to remain the same despite the passage of time and changes in the place where the action occurs?

Discussion of 'What do you do?' (p. 32)

1. *Clear.* This description of John's restless behaviour is expressed in terms that can be measured (in number of moves out of his seat over a period of time).

2. *Not Clear.* The word 'naughty' has too many different interpretations.

3. *Not Clear.* 'Happily' is a subjective description which does not tell us what was actually happening, and cannot be measured or compared with a future or past occasion.

4. *Not Clear.* What is appropriate for one family may not

be so for another, and again we are not told what actually happened.

5. *Clear.* As long as we can agree on what we mean by crying – most people can!

6. *Not Clear.* The word 'tantrum' does not tell us what Kathy actually did; we need to know what actions the tantrum consisted of.

Follow-up quiz

Decide whether the following are clear or not clear:

1. Alice's teacher reported that she answered five times during the reading lesson without raising her head.

2. Bill observed that four people entered the room after the meeting had started.

3. Susan's teacher said that the most important aim of the Literature course was the development of an appreciation of poetry.

4. Henry played about and tried to get attention while his parents talked to their visitors.

5. Setting down your observations

What do you do?

Choose from A, B or C below the information you would record about the following four examples of problem behaviour.

A *How often* a particular action occurs.
B *How long* the activity goes on.
C *How much of his time* your child spends on the activity.

1. Your child calls out for you regularly when you have left him in bed at night.
   Would you record A, B or C?

2. Your child never seems to do what he is told.
   Would you record A, B or C?

3. Your child is always leaving clothes around the house.
   Would you record A, B or C?

4. An extreme example: your child is restless, his concentration is poor, and you are worried about his ability to persevere with a task.
   Would you record A, B or C.

Once the need to observe and describe accurately is recognized there is one further step to take in order to achieve a

Answers: 1: B; 2: C; 3: A; 4: B

firm base from which to influence your children's behaviour. Unless some record is made of what a child is doing before you try to make changes, you are unlikely to be sure later of how successful you have been. So records of before, during and after are necessary. The recording methods suggested here will also help parents to put their child's behaviour problem into perspective, so that, perhaps for the first time, they can see it as others might do. Most parents are so involved with their children that they fail to see obvious connections between their own and their children's ways of doing things. This chapter will also consider some other reasons for observing and recording your children's actions and why it is so important in dealing with many behaviour problems.

Collecting information

When descriptions of what children do are clear you can begin to record some of the characteristics of their actions. There are many ways of recording for different situations. Before we go on to consider what and how to record in various situations we must first know a few of the most useful methods.

1. How often

Recording how often a child does something in a given period of time is the most generally useful procedure. Some activities may occur very frequently; for example, hitting, biting, screaming, kicking, or throwing things. Others may be a problem because they occur infrequently: putting toys away, playing with other children, etc. Recording how often an action occurs is appropriate for both types of problem.

When counting how often a child does something it is

important that the activity should not be dependent on what the *parents* do. For example, if you are trying to find out how disobedient your child is being, counting how often he follows instructions may be misleading, since this will depend also on the number of instructions that you give him. You may also unwittingly give only instructions that you know your child will follow, or on the other hand only those that you know he usually disobeys. Your recordings may then tell you more about your own habits of giving instructions than about your child's response to them.

Counting *how often* your child does something is most conveniently recorded as follows. List the clearly defined actions of the child on separate lines at the top of a sheet. Then, for each day of the week, make a mark for each time an action occurs. Here is an example of the method in use.

Week of 20–26 January, 197…	*Name of child JOHN*
Action to be observed	*Duration of recording*
1. Hitting other children	All day
2. Screaming	All day
3. Throwing objects (other than at appropriate play time)	All day

---

Monday 20 January	Total	Comments
1. HHH HHH HHH	1. __15__	Ordinary day
2. HHH HHH 11	2. __12__	
3. HHH 11	3. __7__	
Tuesday 21 January		
1. HHH HHH 111	1. __13__	Afternoon out in
2. HHH 1	2. __6__	the park
3. 111	3. __3__	
Wednesday 22 January		
1. HHH HHH HHH 111	1. __18__	Visitors with young
2. HHH HHH HHH HHH HHH HHH HHH	2. __35__	child
3. HHH HHH 1	3. __11__	

Children and parents

Thursday 23 January
1. ~~HHI~~ ~~HHI~~ 1   1. __11__   Ordinary day
2. ~~HHI~~ ~~HHI~~ 1   2. __11__
3. ~~HHI~~ 111   3. __8__

Friday 24 January
1. ~~HHI~~ ~~HHI~~ ~~HHI~~ ~~HHI~~ 11   1. __22__   Ordinary day
2. ~~HHI~~ ~~HHI~~ 1111   2. __14__
3. 1111   3. __4__

Saturday 25 January
1. ~~HHI~~ ~~HHI~~ ~~HHI~~ 111   1. __18__   Went into the city
2. 1111   2. __4__   to go shopping
3. ~~HHI~~ 1   3. __6__

Sunday 26 January
1. ~~HHI~~ ~~HHI~~ ~~HHI~~ 1   1. __16__   Went to church
2. 1111   2. __4__   and out to dinner
3. 11   3. __2__

The results for Monday show that John has hit fifteen times, screamed twelve times and thrown things seven times. You can see how he did on the other days. Already, you begin to get some idea of the frequency and extent of the problem, and may see what is influencing it.

2. How long

Recording how long an activity goes on can be used with 'good' and 'bad' behaviour. For example, you can record the period of concentration on one task during homework, or the length of time spent crying in a temper outburst. The goal in changing these activities is to increase or decrease the time they last. When recording, simply note how long each action lasts. For example, Bernard had difficulty in getting ready for school on time each morning. He was too slow, and would get involved in books and games and forget what he was supposed to be doing. Bernard's mother was fed up with having to hurry him along each day. She decided that before trying to do anything else, she should make a record of how long it took him to get ready. The recording for one week looked as follows:

Week of 19–23 July, 197...

Action to be observed	*Period of observation*
Time to get ready for school	Mornings

Monday 7.00–8.35 a.m. = 95 mins.	*Comments*
Tuesday 7.00–8.50 a.m. =110 mins.	Found Bernard playing with a puzzle in his room.
Wednesday 7.00–9.00 a.m. =120 mins.	Bernard playing with the dog.
Thursday 7.10–8.30 a.m. = 80 mins.	
Friday 7.00–8.40 a.m. =100 mins.	Bernard in bathroom – playing with toy boats in sink.

These observations of Bernard for one week show his slowness and why he is slower at some times than at others. Obviously, other information about dressing, breakfast and Bernard's mother's actual methods of trying to speed him up would be helpful. However, even with this bare recording of time taken in the mornings his mother will know later without any doubt whether the new method of encouraging him has shortened the time he takes each morning.

3. How much

Here you record the proportion of time spent on a particular activity out of the total possible time. For instance, to show how well your child cooperates within the family list a number of common requests or instructions which you are likely to give on most days. With a young child, you may need to set up a situation specifically to test his willingness to comply or be helpful, such as playing a particular game. The same set of instructions to the child are used each time and a time limit is set for the completion of each direction. The time limit will vary with the type of instruction or request.

Another example will help to make this clear. Mandy's parents complained that she had to be asked to do things several times before taking any notice. For instance, she took no notice at first when asked to finish playing and come indoors; she ignored them when they asked her to get ready for dinner, so that she was always late, and she delayed going to bed until told many times. The following record could be made of the number of occasions Mandy responded first time to being asked to do something.

From this we can see that Mandy was always willing to go to the shop (1), but only once came in from play (2) when first required. She did not often respond first time to being asked to go to bed (4) or put away her clothes (5) either. She would usually help to lay the table (3) – but two out of three times she did not do it properly. For some reason she was particularly cooperative on the evening of 21 January, and one would have to look at the special circumstances of that evening to think of why this should be so.

Recording the proportion of wanted to unwanted reactions is more frequently used when you are trying to teach a child something new, or are helping him with a particular difficulty such as a speech problem. In these situations the instructor or parent gives the child some kind of instruction and waits for him to respond. The child may react as you want, fail to respond or make a good attempt which is not quite right.

Let us look at an example of the use of this procedure in helping a child to say words clearly. Philip had a mild speech

Response to Directions

Directions	20 Jan. a.m.	p.m.	21 Jan. a.m.	p.m.	22 Jan. a.m.	p.m.	23 Jan. a.m.	p.m.
1. Please go to the shop for me. (15 minutes)		+		+		+		+
2. Stop playing and come indoors now. (5 minutes)	0	0	0	+	0	0	0	0
3. Please help me lay the table. (1 minute)		—		+		—		0
4. Up you go to bed now. (5 minutes)		0		+		0		0
5. Please put your clothes away. (1 minute)	0	0	0	+	0	+	+	0

0 : did not respond; + : responded as requested; — : responded, but not correctly.

problem, and a record was made on ten occasions in a day of his imitation of three family names.

The information shows that Philip is at this time able to get these words right about thirty to forty per cent of the time, and it will not be difficult to see when improvement is made.

These are some of the simple recording procedures. You need to know what your child is doing and what effects you are having on his behaviour if you are to alter things in the

Children and parents

Imitating names: *20 January 197...*

	1	2	3	4	5	6	7	8	9	10	%
'Mummy'	+	+	0	—	/	/	/	+	/	+	40
'Daddy'	0	0	/	/	0	/	+	/	+	+	30
'John'	0	/	/	/	+	+	/	+	0	+	40

+ : Correct; / : Near miss; — : Incorrect; 0 : No response.

future. But before you rush ahead and look, there are one or two more important points. First, recording children's specific actions is for most parents a new experience. Do not be discouraged if it seems too much trouble or too difficult at first – just give the method a chance to show that it can be useful. Second, some parents run into difficulties because they want to get down to changing what their child is doing immediately. We advise you first to evaluate what is taking place by considering your own interaction with your child; you are now able to record what your child is doing, but you should also make a note of:

i. *The place where* the child does the things that you are concerned about. For example, some children are difficult only at home, others at school or nursery. Some children are a problem in both places. The setting in which the behaviour occurs is obviously important in deciding what to do about it.

ii. *The circumstances or conditions* also vary. For example, some children are particularly difficult when visitors are present, or when it is time for them to help in the house. By noting these circumstances regularly you can get to know what usually starts off the problem.

48

iii. *What happens after* he acts in the way you are concerned about. This has an important bearing on whether he will act in that way again. You will remember from earlier chapters the importance of reinforcing the 'appropriate' or wanted actions of children. You may also recall that unexpected things can be reinforcing under some circumstances – a child may actually provoke a spanking if this is the only way he can gain his father's attention; children sometimes steal not because they want the stolen objects, but because they get a great deal of attention from friends for such an action. By taking particular notice of what you do in response to your child's behaviour, you will often find that you are giving him attention in a way that perpetuates problems. In many families the very act of observing and recording has either shown parents that their child's problem behaviour is not of great significance at all, or helped them to see quickly what they need to do to help the child get over it. However, some problems are not so easily resolved, and it is in these situations that the recording is particularly valuable.

Once you have decided which activity you are concerned about, the next step is to choose the appropriate recording procedure. If, for example, you are recording outbursts of screaming by your child, you may be interested in how often and how long he screams. But parents cannot go round all day with paper and pencil in their hands. What can you do to make recording practicable?

First you must decide when and how to record. If the screaming episodes occur infrequently but last a long time when they do, it may be sufficient in the first place to record how long the outburst lasts. This type of screaming should probably be recorded for the whole day, with a note of the time each episode starts and stops; you will also know at the end of the day how often he has screamed. If the screaming occurs in short but frequent bouts it is only necessary to record a sample over a shorter period of time. Notes can be made during one particular hour each day, and if the information is gathered and recorded in a consistent manner it should reflect the general pattern of the screaming. It is obviously helpful if you have some way of timing accurately, and also if you have some sort of counting-aid such as a shopping-list indicator or any other gadget which enables you to keep a score of the number of times the screaming or other activity occurs.

Lastly, do not forget to take a record of your child's problem behaviour as it is *before* you try to make any changes in it. You should continue the record until you are sure you have got a representative picture of what usually happens. In other words, make sure you do not record his activities only on some unusual day or special occasion. It is always better if your child is not aware that you are noting his actions at this stage in particular.

You may find the following recording procedure useful –

and it may be the only one you have time for in a busy daily schedule. We call this an interval recording procedure. It works quite simply. To explain it we will refer again to John, the first example in this chapter (p. 43). Do you remember the rate at which John screamed? The actual totals for each day of the week were 12, 6, 35, 11, 14, 4 and 4. Consider the difficulty of marking or scoring each of the 35 screams John emitted on Wednesday when company was present. His mother was trying to cook, talk to her friends, keep peace in the house, and so on, and meanwhile trying to record. It's quite a problem. Suppose in this situation the mother decided not to record each instance of screaming (she just didn't have time), but only to record whether, during any given half-hour, John did or did not scream. Whether John screamed once or ten times in a given half-hour did not matter, it was always scored as one. Here is how the information would look:

Wednesday	Screamed	Did not scream
7.00– 7.30 a.m.		×
7.30– 8.00 a.m.		×
8.00– 8.30 a.m.	×	
8.30– 9.00 a.m.	×	
9.00– 9.30 a.m.		×
9.30–10.00 a.m.	×	
10.00–10.30 a.m.		×
10.30–11.00 a.m.		×
11.00–11.30 a.m.	×	
11.30–12.00 a.m.		×
12.00–12.30 a.m.	×	
12.30– 1.00 p.m.	×	
1.00– 1.30 p.m.	×	
1.30– 2.00 p.m.	×	
2.00– 2.30 p.m.	×	
2.30– 3.00 p.m.	×	

Children and parents

Wednesday	Screamed	Did not scream
3.00– 3.30 p.m.	×	
3.30– 4.00 p.m.	×	
4.00– 4.30 p.m.	×	
4.30– 5.00 p.m.	×	
5.00– 5.30 p.m.	×	
5.30– 6.00 p.m.	×	
6.00– 6.30 p.m.	×	
6.30– 7.00 p.m.	×	
7.00– 7.30 p.m.	×	
7.30– 8.00 p.m.	×	
8.00– 8.30 p.m.	×	
8.30– 9.00 p.m.		×
9.00– 9.30 p.m.		×
9.30–10.00 p.m.		×
	—	—
Total	21 +	9
	—	—

A shortened version of the record could look like this.

John – screaming – Wednesday – half-hour intervals

	a.m.						p.m.						
	7	8	9	10	11	12	1	2	3	4	5	6	7	8	9
1st half-hour	×				×	×	×	×	×	×	×	×	×	×	
2nd half-hour	×	×				×	×	×	×	×	×	×	×		

By this system John's screaming would have scored for the seven days as 8, 4, 21, 7, 10, 3 and 4.

If the mother had decided to mark down only every hour whether John did or didn't scream, she would have counted 5, 3, 12, 3, 6, 2, and 3 for each of the days. Counting just morning, afternoon and evening gave her less information.

Setting down your observations

Let's compare what the mother gathered by the different procedures to determine which one would give us enough information about what is going on but would still not be too difficult and time-consuming.

	Total count	½-hour intervals	1-hour intervals	morning afternoon night
Monday	12	8	5	2
Tuesday	6	4	3	2
Wednesday	35	21	12	3
Thursday	11	7	3	2
Friday	14	10	6	2
Saturday	4	3	2	2
Sunday	4	4	3	2

Later on in the chapter we will show this information on a graph so you can see what it looks like. The point to be made is that recording every half-hour or every hour seems to give us sufficient information on the pattern of behaviour. Recording every occurrence is probably not necessary, though there will be some situations where you will want to do this. It will take some practice on your part to find out what works best for you.

Graphing

It is easier to see what the information you have gathered means if you can bring it all together and summarize it. The clearest way to do this is to represent what happens as a graph, so that you can see at a glance how you are progressing. Simple ways to make the graphs will be described in this section, and examples will be given of each type of recorded information. Plotting the day-to-day recording is really quite straightforward.

Basically two sorts of information are needed. The first is "when" the child did whatever you are concerned about,

and the second is "how much" he did. It will be easier to see this with an example.

Draw a line across a piece of paper and mark it off into sections, which will represent the days in this instance.

| 1 | 2 | 3 | 4 | 5 | 6 | 7 | 8 | 9 | 10 | 11 | 12 | 13 | 14 |

We now have two weeks on which we can record what has happened. Next we can draw a vertical line marked off into

different sections which will represent 'how much' of the
child's behaviour took place during each of the days. The
numbering will vary, depending upon what you are recording.

Here is an example. Let's take John's screaming as the
behaviour. 'How much' screaming is best measured by the
number of screams occurring in a period of time (a one-day
time sample is used here). For John's screaming behaviour
we have given you several versions of the vertical line.

We now want to combine the information of 'when' and
'how much' in a summarizing graph, which in this case will
be able to show the number of screams per day over a period
of two weeks. Remember that the rate of John's screaming
for the first week was 12, 6, 35, 11, 14, 4, 4, on the seven
consecutive days.

Start by drawing and marking off a horizontal and a
vertical line in the way we have just described. To score
(plot) a point, look at when John screamed (Monday –
Day 1) and at how often he screamed (12 times on Day 1).
Now draw a line up from Day 1 and another line across from
12 (the number of times he screamed that day). The point at
which these lines meet is the correct location for this score.

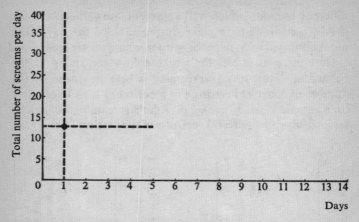

Now repeat this process for each subsequent day. You will soon manage without the additional lines, and then need only draw in the points representing the number of screaming attacks on each day.

Once you have the points plotted you can join them up and get a picture representing the changes in number of

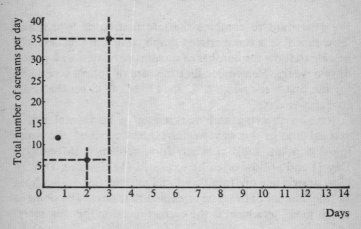

screams from day to day. A picture of John's screams over a week is shown thus:

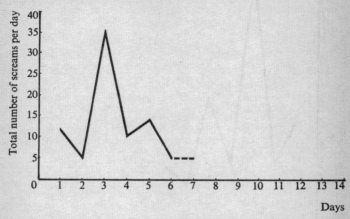

The same information measured by half-hour, by hour, and by morning, afternoon, and evening intervals would be graphed as follows:

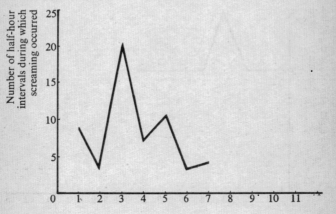

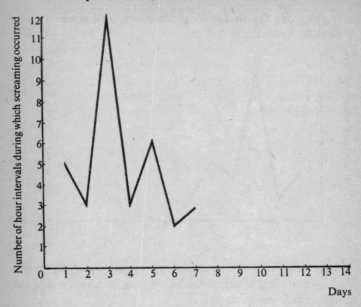

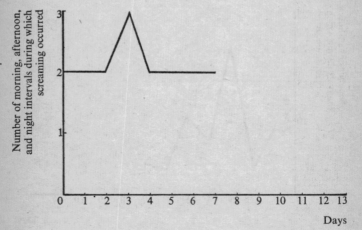

Notice that the easiest method of recording which still gives sufficient information is the one-hour interval method. However, this may not be the best procedure for other behaviour problems. Let us look at some different examples.

Before trying to change his way of behaving, John's mother made a note of the number of times he hit his brother and sister.

20 Jan. – 15 times
21 „ – 13 „
22 „ – 18 „
23 „ – 11 „
24 „ – 22 „
25 „ – 18 „

On the graph it looked like this:

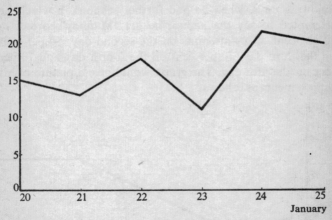

The example given on p. 45 of how long Bernard took to get ready for school in the mornings would be represented by the first graph on the next page.

When Philip (see pp. 46-8) was tested on his ability to say three family names, he got 'Mummy' correct in 40 per cent of his attempts at the name. Let us imagine that on the

59

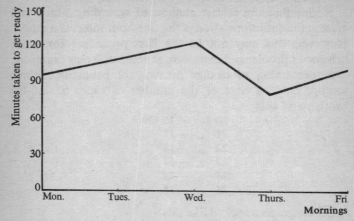

following days, when he had further sessions in which he attempted to say the names, he got 'Mummy' correct in 30 per cent of his attempts on the second day, 50 per cent on the third day, 70 per cent on the fourth day and 70 per cent on the fifth day. The graph would give a picture of his achievements as follows:

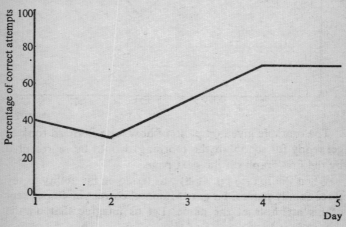

One final useful idea to keep the picture clear is to draw a line marking off the record of your child's behaviour at the point where you start to make changes. Another sample graph will make this clear:

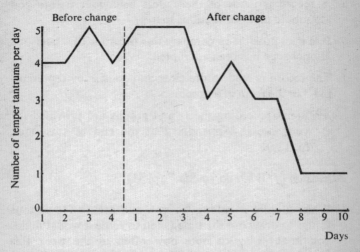

As we have indicated earlier, the collecting and graphing of information on your child's behaviour can be an illuminating experience which may be rewarding in itself. In any event it is the only fair foundation on which to build up new skills for your children and help teach them satisfactory ways of adapting to their world.

Summary of main points in the chapter

1. Once your child's problems have been defined, you can start recording his behaviour regularly.

2. Parents most often count the number of times their child does something.

3. However, they may also be interested in how long he carries on an activity, or in

4. What proportion of time he reacts in a particular way.

5. A record is made of the child's behaviour before you attempt to make alterations to it.

6. It is then possible to compare this record with a later one after change has been attempted.

7. The record is made more clear and concise by representing it in the form of a graph.

Note: Blank recording-sheets and graphs are provided for your use in Appendix 2 at the end of this book (p. 129).

Discussion of 'What do you do?' (p. 41)

1. When a child is calling for you and asking for various things to draw out the time taken to settle down at night, you might wish to note how often in the week this happens. But your aim will be to reduce gradually the amount of delaying tactics each night, so a more useful measure of this would be to time how long it goes on each evening, or on selected evenings.

(Answer: B)

2. Although he *never* seems to do what you ask, there will be times when he is more willing than others. The occasions when he does comply, as well as the times when he ignores or refuses, should be recorded so that you can see the proportion of your total requests for help or cooperation to which he responds.

(Answer: C)

3. 'Untidiness' should always be defined specifically, as in

this example; where it consists of leaving clothes around the house.

The degree of untidiness can probably best be measured by noting how often it occurs, and this might be most easily assessed by counting the number of articles of clothing scattered about throughout the day.

(Answer: A)

4. In the case of concentration and attention, the aim will be to lengthen slowly the period your child can persevere with a task or game without being distracted to some other activity. You therefore need an estimate of how long he can concentrate in the first place, before trying to extend this.

(Answer: B)

Follow-up quiz

Exercise 1.

Use one of the following words or phrases to fill in the blanks in this advice about recording and graphing:

A: before change;
B: how often;
C: what;
D: proportion;
E: how long;
F: when.

When you are checking whether your child does what you ask him to do, recording (1) .... would not be appropriate since this depends on the number and type of instructions you give him. The (2) .... of instructions he obeys is much more valid.

Children and parents

Before you try to influence your child's problem behaviour it is advisable to record his actions in the period (3) .... From this you will be able to assess changes later.

The graphs parents make help to summarize their recorded observations. The line going up the left side of the chart tells (4) .... you are recording, and the line across the bottom of the chart tells (5) .... things happened.

(Answers at end of quiz, p. 66.)

Exercise 2.

Fill in the graph on the blank form below with the information from the following example:

Gary, an eight-year-old, was a very quiet, timid child and did not play much with other children at his school. His teacher was concerned about this and decided to record the amount of time he spent with other children. From 10 to 11 a.m. each morning for a week, a member of the staff made a note whenever Gary talked to another child or participated in a group activity. The record showed that on Monday, Gary played or talked with other children twice. On the following four days, the number of occasions time was spent with other children during this hour was one, three, none and one. After this 'before change' period of recording the staff successfully encouraged him to mix more with other children, so that the following week Gary joined in with other children three, six, five, seven and nine times.

Complete the graph below to show these recorded observations clearly.

Name_____ Action Recorded_____ Place_____

Time of recording _____

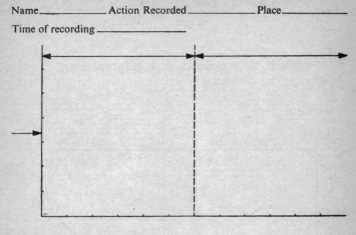

(Answers at end of quiz, p. 66)

Children and parents

Answers

Exercise 1.

1. how often; 2. proportion; 3. before change;
4. what;   5. when.

Exercise 2.

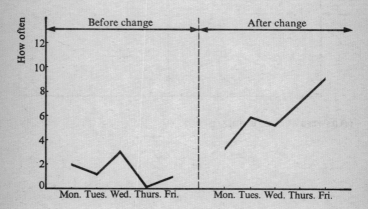

6. Do you need to punish?

What do you do?

Would you say the following statements are true or false?

1. Punishment (scolding or smacking) of children is rarely used by parents.

....

2. Punishing children is the most effective way of helping them to achieve long-lasting control over their ways of behaving.

....

3. When a child does something wrong, the most effective way to teach him not to behave like that is to make sure he does not get any gratification from his actions or to prevent things that he likes from happening.

....

4. Children become emotionally disturbed if parents stop giving attention to behaviour they do not want to encourage and start to reward different ways of behaving.

....

5. Reinforcing children's 'good' behaviour by giving atten-

67

tion to and taking more interest in it is the way to teach them to do things you like.

. . . .

It has been emphasized over and over again in this book that reinforcing children's 'good' behaviour by giving attention, praise and affection or rewards is ultimately the way to get them to behave in that way more frequently.

Many minor problems, such as temper outbursts when children cannot get their own way, or provocative swearing to test out your reaction, can be reduced or stopped altogether if parents and others are able to take no notice of them for a while. However, there are some acts such as destructive or very aggressive behaviour that cannot be ignored. It is the purpose of this chapter to present effective methods to control these and other sorts of behaviour which demand attention and need to be changed.

Punishment?

Most parents use punishments of various sorts to try to control the behaviour of their children. What are the usual effects of this?

A six-year-old boy playing with his sister begins to quarrel and fight. They are told to separate or play together without fighting, but the boy hits out and hurts his sister. The immediate reaction of many parents, in their annoyance, would be to smack him; thus the immediate consequence for the child of hitting his sister is the punishing smack. This is the opposite to reinforcing an action by giving attention,

Answers: 1: False; 2: False; 3: True; 4: False; 5: True

praise or rewards immediately after it occurs. Punishment means that the consequences of the action are the sorts of things children would rather not experience. They are certainly not things that normally serve as reinforcements to actions.

The effect of punishment is often immediate and sometimes dramatic. The unwanted activity usually stops quickly – no wonder parents learn to use shouting, smacking and other punishments so often. However, their frequent use, besides being distasteful to most parents, also has a number of undesirable effects.

1. It is very shortlived in effect, as most people learn eventually. Unless the punishment is extremely severe the child's behaviour will revert to its earlier form soon after the punishment is no longer in effect. All that happens when parents punish is that the child's behaviour is temporarily suppressed – it is not permanently changed.

2. Punishment itself tends to escalate: the child repeats the undesired behaviour, the parents repeat the punishment slightly more harshly. This again is only temporarily effective, and soon the behaviour occurs again. More and more forceful measures are needed each time, for what is actually happening is that the child is being trained to withstand increasingly severe punishments.

3. At the same time parents are drawn into using punishments more frequently. They get temporary relief from the child's 'naughty' behaviour each time they punish him, and so they learn to use this method of control, often to the exclusion of more long-lasting methods.

4. The effect of (2) and (3) is that the child's relationship with his parent deteriorates, as it is based on punitive control rather than encouragement and positive training.

This often produces emotional reactions which may become more serious than the original problem.

5. The child 'learns' from the parents' example to use aggressive behaviour to get his way with others.

I hereby sentence you to 20 days bed and no T.V.

In general, great caution must be exercised with punishment. Little is known about its effects in any particular circumstances, other than that it produces immediate but only temporary modification in behaviour. A school teacher who has a very noisy class may find that by shouting at the whole group he can produce a period of quietness. After a while, however, the chatter and noisy movement start again so that another shout is necessary. After the first few weeks of the term, the teacher is yelling at the class more and more frequently and loudly. The short period of silence after each shouting reinforces the teacher's shouting, and he thus learns to yell at the class more often and more strongly only to get a temporary benefit.

What you can do instead of smacking or shouting

1. Reinforce alternative ways of behaving

Young children when first walking and able to explore their house sometimes take an interest in electric plugs and sockets in the wall. Parents naturally pull them away hurriedly and sometimes give a slap if they continue to handle the wires or plug. This has an immediate effect, but it does not encourage children to take less interest in electric plugs. The parent could also say suddenly and assertively, 'No, John!' This would have the effect of a mild punishment initially. If John was, at the same time, given something similarly intricate as an alternative to play with and given attention when he played with it, he would be further encouraged away from electric plugs and sockets. Through this combination of mild punishment and reinforced alternative activity the child will learn more quickly to play with other things, rather than electric devices.

In other situations which are not dangerous or serious punishment in any form is out of place. Parents then have to take care that their child's unwanted behaviour is not inadvertently being rewarded by paying special attention to it. Instead you can deliberately reinforce, by attention or reward, some other activity of your child which is incompatible with the behaviour you are trying to discourage. A fidgety girl had got into the habit of picking at tissues, handkerchiefs, the edges of clothes or other fabrics, whenever she was not doing anything else. Punishment was inappropriate for no real damage occurred. The fidgeting and picking was ignored by her parents, and her mother taught her knitting and embroidery, which fitted in with her interest in design. Both parents quite deliberately showed interest in the knitting and encouraged it further by praising the finished articles. Quite soon many spare moments of the girl's leisure time were spent knitting, and she stopped picking.

This method of decreasing unwanted ways of behaviour by encouraging alternative or incompatible activities is obviously easier said than done. It sometimes requires a good deal of ingenuity and patience, neither of which are necessary when delivering punishment. This is probably one of the main reasons for the widespread use of punishment. Reinforcing alternative or incompatible activities has, however, several advantages: the side-effects of punishment are avoided; the delay in effect of merely ignoring the unwanted behaviour does not occur – it can be effective immediately, completely and permanently. Children can be taught desirable ways of behaving at the same time that the undesirable ones are eliminated; indeed, unless they have an alternative activity which gains them the attention or other rewards they previously got for their 'bad' behaviour, punishment will usually have no long-lasting effect.

2. 'Cooling-down' or 'Think' time

This is the equivalent of the 'Go to your room' method used by many parents. It must be used with caution. If you send a child to his own room as a form of punishment he may associate that place with 'bad' behaviour and punishment, which is obviously undesirable. The idea behind the 'Cooling-down' or 'Think' time approach is to reduce any possible reinforcement of his 'bad' behaviour by parents or others in his surroundings. This can be achieved most simply with young children by turning your attention persistently away from your child when he is being provocative or excessively demanding. In a sense, this presentation of the side of your face instead of your full attention subjects the child to a period of isolation from your interest.

With an older child in a rage, it is sometimes necessary to allow him to calm down away from the possible inadvertent encouragement of those around him. Sending or moving him without fuss or discussion into another ordinary room (making sure it is not the one with your favourite display of china!) will often suffice. Leave him in the room until he quietens down a little, letting him come back as soon as he shows signs of calming. Otherwise, the period there should be fairly constant, only one or two minutes for young children, or up to ten minutes for older children. It is important that the whole procedure should not become a game; discussion and explanation of why you are doing it should be left until later when your child is back to ordinary ways of behaving again, and should centre on what he was doing which caused you to move him out of the room. Do not give special attention to the child immediately after the period, but do reinforce the first indications of 'good' behaviour in any form. It must be emphasized that this method should *only* be used if some particularly undesirable behaviour is occurring; it must never be used just because he is being a nuisance, is in your way or is getting on your nerves. This 'Cooling-down' or 'Think' time is a specific method to help children to gain self-control, and must be used consistently at the very time the activity occurs or immediately after.

Children and parents

The most important element in this or any of the other procedures described here is that you should, as far as is humanly possible, be consistent in the way you react to your child's behaviour – both from one day to another and from parent to parent. We often vary in what we say to our children or how we respond to their behaviour, depending more on how we are feeling at that particular time than on what the children are actually doing. If we have had an argument with someone else or if we have been upset or depressed by some other event we are more likely to snap at the children or take too little notice of them when they are needing our attention. Equally common is the tendency for one parent not to support what the other has said or done. This can happen because one has not found out what the other has already said when their child makes demands on them, or because the parents do not agree on what their child should or should not do anyway. Most children will begin to take advantage of this situation and play off one parent against the other. Whatever your ideas about children's development and behaviour, discuss them with your husband or wife and work out a common policy. Then stick together, support one another, and try to react to your child's behaviour rather than your own mood. Consistency is the golden rule for parents and those working with children.

Discussion of 'What do you do?' (p. 67)

1. *False*. Most parents use some form of punishment or threat of punishment to control their children's behaviour. Punishment works initially and thus only rewards the *parent* for using it.

2. *False*. Only very severe punishment has long-lasting

74

effects, and this is damaging in itself. Punishment often produces emotional reactions in children and should be avoided whenever possible. Other procedures such as reinforcement of alternative behaviour are advised.

3. *True*. The 'Cooling-down' or 'Think' time method has been shown to be effective when other procedures have failed. It must, however, be used sparingly and consistently for specific behaviour problems.

4. *False*. Children and adults react to the cessation of rewards for a particular activity by gradually changing to alternative actions which are rewarded in some way. This process does not entail emotional disturbance.

5. *True*. Reinforcing what a child does well is positive and avoids the problems associated with punishment.

Follow-up quiz

In the following examples underline the appropriate word from the alternatives provided:

Example 1.

Ann constantly interrupted when her mother was speaking on the telephone. Her mother was always annoyed with Ann for this behaviour, but without effect. The reprimands were not severe, and the attention given on these occasions was actually rewarding to Ann.

One day Ann's mother decided to ignore her daughter completely at these times. She found that Ann was (1. worse; better) for a few days. Eventually the little girl learned that she was not going to get any more attention for behaving in such a fashion and the number of times she interrupted her mother on the telephone (2. increased; decreased).

Example 2.

Alice did not have any real speech problem, but she had got into the habit of mumbling when she spoke. Even though her mother often did not understand what Alice had said, she usually replied 'Yes dear!' whenever Alice mumbled something. Alice mumbled a great deal at this time.

Once she had recognized what was happening, Alice's mother decided to remain silent whenever her daughter mumbled. In the next two weeks Alice's mumbling became (3. more; less) frequent, and her speech (4. more; less) clear. If her mother again started to say 'yes dear' whenever Alice mumbled, mumbling by Alice would (5. increase; decrease).

Example 3.

All day there had been a great deal of noise at work. When father came home at the end of the day, all the children rushed up yelling 'Daddy! Daddy!' and complaining about one another's behaviour. Daddy soon shouted 'shut up!' very loudly. For the next fifteen minutes there was silence.

In the future their father shouted 'shut up!' in this and other sorts of situations more frequently. His shouting 'shut up!' loudly was (6. reinforcing; punishing) to the children's noisy clamouring, and they therefore became quiet for a while. However, this effect on the children's behaviour tended to (7. reinforce; punish) their father's shouting 'shut up!' and therefore he did this more often.

Example 4.

It was very important to nine-year-old Bill that he should be regarded by his friends as tough and 'one of the boys'. He was also very unkempt in his appearance. His teacher, in the hope of encouraging him to take more care of his appearance in the future, decided to reward him with praise when he came to school looking less scruffy than usual. His teacher would then draw attention to his appearance and praise him for it. The result was a deterioration on the following days in Bill's appearance, which seemed for some time after to be deliberately dishevelled. For Bill's dressing more carefully, the praise he got in front of the class was (8. reinforcing; punishing). Bill hated to be made the centre of attention. The teacher had made a mistake in this case.

Example 5.

Christopher was a constant problem in his class. He pulled girls' hair, never stayed in his seat for more than five minutes, and was very noisy most of the day. Instead of trying to punish Christopher for this behaviour as others had done, his new teacher decided to reinforce any work done by Christopher by rewarding him with a good deal of personal attention and praise whenever he made any effort to work. As a result Christopher began to do more work in class. As the amount of work he did increased, his behaviour in class (9. remained the same; became better; became worse). It was not possible for Christopher to work harder and still be as 'bad' in his class as he used to be. The two ways of behaving are (10. compatible; incompatible).

Answers: 1: Worse; 2: decreased; 3: less; 4: more; 5: increase; 6: punishing; 7: reinforce; 8: punishing; 9: became better; 10: incompatible

7. Learning new ways of behaving

What do you do?

1. You want your nine-year-old son to learn to use a saw safely. He is keen to make some wooden structure and has already tried the saw, but with disappointing results. Would you:

A Demonstrate how you should hold and use a saw, and then say 'that's right, well done' and praise his work as he tries to do the same and gets better and better.

B Let him gradually find out his own way of handling the saw.

C Keep an eye on the way he uses the saw and, if he holds and uses it correctly and safely, say 'that's right, well done' and praise his work.

2. Your seven-year-old daughter, who is rather timid, has only a short walk to school, but even so has always had your company. When you move to a house further away from the school she has to go by bus, though she has not previously travelled alone on a bus. You want her to gain more independence and to go to school by herself. Supposing there are no busy roads she will have to cross at either end of the journey, make a list of the steps you would take to teach her eventually to travel unaccompanied to school.

Answers: 1: A; 2: see p. 82.

So far the emphasis has been on changing already established ways of behaving. In this chapter we shall concentrate on ways of getting children to behave in *new* ways which they have never previously learned. There are two main methods of approaching this task; they are usually called 'shaping' and 'modelling'. In practice these are nearly always combined to some extent.

Shaping

We know that when we want someone to do something more often we should reinforce that particular activity with attention, praise, rewards, and so on. If you want your child to behave in some new way it is usually impractical to wait for it to happen spontaneously in order to be able to encourage its repetition by reinforcement. In this sort of situation a 'shaping' method is needed. Shaping consists of reinforcing anything that is near to what you wish your child to learn, then gradually reinforcing closer and closer approximations to it.

First you must define clearly what it is that you want your child to learn to do. Secondly you need to find something he does that in some way resembles it, and then reinforce this action whenever he does it. As he begins to do it more often you should no longer reinforce it every time, but only when the action resembles the desired behaviour more closely than before. The process is repeated over and over again until finally your child will have learnt what you set out to teach him and, with further reinforcement, this can be established as a habit. This is very much like 'hunt-the-thimble'; parents reinforce the child, gradually getting closer to the goal by saying 'You're getting warmer', and ignoring movements away or saying 'You're getting colder'. Shaping is often a very slow process in everyday experience because you have to wait for the child to make the first move. Thus, shaping is nearly always combined with modelling.

Modelling

Relying on 'shaping' methods alone for teaching new skills or ways of behaving means a long wait for results, If, however, the new skill or activity is shown to the child so that he has something to try to imitate, the process is greatly speeded up. This is 'modelling' – providing a 'model' for the child to copy. Teachers frequently use modelling when teaching techniques that a class of children have not yet experienced – 'Watch how I do it!' 'Do it like this!' Parents automatically model new actions to show their young children how to do things, or point to the behaviour of others as an example of how to carry out some task. Leading a child directly through the steps of a new activity is also a form of modelling. For example, when teaching a child to hold a pencil for writing, the teacher may place the pencil correctly in the child's hand and hold it herself at the same time, helping to make the first movements. Usually when the child gets the idea and makes a good effort at getting the right position for writing, the teacher will say 'that's good!' or give some other encouragement. In this way 'shaping', by reinforcing the closer approximations to the desired goal, is also being used.

One of the important things affecting the extent to which a child will imitate is what happens to the person acting as the model as a result of what he does. If your child sees that a certain way of behaving clearly leads to some kind of satisfaction, he is likely to act in that way when he gets the opportunity. In the same way, a child may also learn undesirable ways of behaving as well as the ones you hope for. In the first few years of life parents are usually the main adult models for their children, so that we all have a good deal of responsibility for the long-lasting patterns of behaviour our children adopt. Brothers and sisters also play an important role as models as time goes by, and later schoolfriends, teachers, other adults, and regular experiences like watching television provide further models of behaviour. Arguments, fights, dishonesty, or any other undesirable activities, particularly if they are seen in some way to 'pay off', serve as models for your children's behaviour just as much as the things you would really like them to learn.

Children and parents

Discussion of 'What do you do?' (p. 78)

1. Your nine-year-old boy would probably make many mistakes, some dangerous, if he were left to find his own way to use the saw (B). Praising him whenever he used it well (C) would be more effective than (B), but if the correct use of the saw were demonstrated to him and then he was praised as he got nearer and nearer to correct handling (A), this would result in the fastest and most accurate learning of the necessary skill. In fact you would have gone through the process of modelling and shaping.

2. The main steps by which you could try and ensure a trouble-free transition from the old way of going to school to the new way by bus are:
   i. Parent accompanies the child on the bus and right up to the school entrance.
   ii. Parent accompanies the child on the bus and to within sight of the school.
   iii. Parent accompanies the child on the bus and stays at the bus stop at the school end of the journey.
   iv. Parent takes the child to the bus stop near home and does not go on the bus.
   v. Parent stays at home.

The process is graded so that each step requires a little more independent effort, and each step is repeated until the child is fairly confident before moving on to the next.

Follow-up quiz

Insert one of the following words in each of the blanks in the example below:

> *praise; praised; reinforced; shaped; model; modelling.*

(Each word may be used more than once.)

Your little boy is learning to eat with a knife and fork after having only used a spoon and fingers previously. He watches you using a knife and fork at dinner and sees that you are able to cut up food into manageable portions and do not need the help of others. Already you are teaching him by (1) .... the new activity he wants to acquire, and he begins to try to use the small knife and fork provided for him. At first he is not very successful and gets frustrated. You then provide a more direct (2) .... by leaning over, placing the knife and fork in his hands in the best grip, and actually making the necessary movements of controlling and cutting by moving his hands with yours. He can see from the experience of using the knife and fork in this way that it gives him the advantages he did not have with his old spoon-and-fingers method. The new way of eating is, therefore, (3) .... both by the advantages it gives him as well as by his desire to do things like his parents and older brother. He eagerly wants to do it himself without help. This time his first attempts with the knife and fork should be (4) .... As he goes on, either at the same meal or on subsequent occasions, you do not continue to (5) .... his eating method unless his technique with the knife and fork has improved a little each time. In this way his manner of eating is gradually being (6) .... towards a competence which is appropriate for his age. It may be necessary to repeat the (7) .... procedure from time to time in order to correct mistakes or as a reminder of the final goal.

This illustration may seem to be complicating what is often a very simple learning process. It is, however, what we find when such a 'simple' process is analysed, and it provides a good example of the way in which new skills and ways of behaving are taught. Much more complex tasks, such as driving a car or engineering techniques, can be learned more efficiently by the use of these basic principles.

8. Making contracts and agreements

What do you do?

1. Your little girl seems to have lost interest in school and stopped trying in her work since moving into her new class. Besides discussing the problem with her new teacher, what would you do at home to try to encourage her back to her former interest in school?

A Praise her when she shows you some good work done at school.

B Give her something she likes when she brings home some good work.

C Start to give her coloured paper stars (like they do at her school) when she has obviously made some effort in her class work; and after she has earned five stars, give her a small prize of something she likes.

D Give stars placed on a chart for trying at school, combined with praise and something she likes for achieving good results (five stars earning this small prize).

2. In coming to an agreement with your child about helping with some jobs in the house, which of the following agreements or contracts would you use?

A 'Patrick, if you are helpful today I will give you a surprise tonight.'

B 'Patrick, if you don't make your bed and clear up your toys today, you won't be allowed to watch television tonight.'

Children and parents

C   'Patrick, if you make your bed today and put your toys away, you can watch the film on television at 7.30 this evening.'

D   'Patrick, clear up your room or you are going to get smacked, and I mean it!'

3. If a parent agreed to the following suggestions or requests from a child, which do you think would make satisfactory agreements or contracts, ensuring that both sides of the arrangement are fulfilled?

A   'I will do my homework, Daddy, when I've watched just one more television programme.'

B   'Daddy, may I go to the cinema this afternoon if I eat my cabbage now?'

C   'Mummy, may I go and play with Colin after I've been to the shops for you?'

D   'Mother, may I invite Sally for tea after I finish helping you with the cleaning?'

Two further procedures can be used in conjunction with those already described to complete the basic list of methods parents will find useful with children.

Reinforcement by the use of tokens

Reinforcement, in the form of things that your child enjoys, increases the likelihood of his behaving again as he did immediately before the reinforcement. One of the goals for a parent or teacher is, therefore, to find things that will act as reinforcement for the activities they wish to encourage. You will probably have had doubts already about giving

Answers: 1: D; 2: C; 3: C and D

86

tangible rewards like sweets or small toys regularly to your children in return for 'good' behaviour from them. It is not always possible or desirable and older children often don't find these things rewarding in any case.

Tokens, as substitutes for other rewards, provide a way of always being ready to reinforce one of the activities of your child. The token may be points, 'stars', counters, beads – anything which can later be counted up and exchanged for something he would really like. They are especially useful when there is little response to praise or other attention, and when the child's motivation to cooperate at home or school is low.

Clearly, with young children in particular, you cannot expect tokens to act as an intermediate step in this way without teaching the child about the system first. When very young children are first given a token it should be exchanged immediately for the reward. This should be done on several occasions before going on gradually to lengthen the interval between giving the token and giving a reward in exchange for it. Eventually you will also be able to teach him that he has to 'earn' a certain specified number of tokens before they can be exchanged.

A token system can be altered to fit the needs of a changing situation. For instance you may:

i. increase or decrease what your child has to do to 'earn' a specified number of tokens.
ii. increase or decrease the number of tokens needed to be exchanged for a reward.
iii. increase or decrease the time-lag before tokens can be exchanged for a reward.

As well as giving out tokens, always show interest in and give praise for your child's achievements, and of course even more so when enough tokens have been gained to exchange for a reward. Eventually it is the goal of the token system, as with any other programme we are describing, to be faded out. This may come about in two ways: the action itself may become rewarding for the child – for example, reinforcing good handwriting by tokens, or any other way, will often lead to the child getting personal satisfaction from his writing; or the activity may become reinforced by its consequences in another setting – for example, reinforcing homework by tokens or other systems will often lead to better work in school, which gets appreciation from the teacher, which in turn reinforces further studying and more improvement in learning. Material rewards are then no longer needed.

Making a contract

In trying to guide their children, adults too often rely on punishment and threats. A parent will tell his child if he does not want to be punished he must behave in certain ways. This is in a sense an attempt by the parent to come to an agreement or make a contract with his child. The contract is that in order *not* to get punished the child must behave in a certain way. For example you might say: 'You won't get any pudding if you don't eat your meat!' This is a very *negative* agreement to try to make – we have seen earlier how punishment can lead to poor or unexpected results. Agreements or contracts should be based on *positive* consequences to be really effective. Thus a teacher might say: 'As soon as you have shown that you have learned this piece of work, you can choose your own activity in the classroom.'

Positive contracts occur in many everyday situations. Most interpersonal activities hinge on positive contracts. Some of these are formal; the parties enter into an agreement in which actions and responsibilities are clearly laid down in detail. Most contracts between individuals, however, are very informal and sometimes not stated. 'Successful' marriages are based on many positive contracts between the partners which provide rewarding consequences for each.

Between parents and children, of course, the agreement may at first be one-sided. A 'statement' is made of the condi-

tions and consequences a parent intends to apply in order to influence the behaviour of his children. Ultimately, however, the intention is to share the agreement and to shift the responsibility on to the child so that he controls some of the consequences of his own actions. For example, the responsible older child eventually makes a contract with himself to do his hour of homework in order to go out or read a novel later. By this time, too, he may be able to understand for himself some of the long-term benefits which come from doing homework.

Reinforcement or rewarding plays a prominent part in contracts, as with other systems. Reinforcement may be in the form of something a child likes: attention, praise, interest, favoured activities, games, watching T.V. and so on. You know the sort of things your own children like. To be effective, however, the rewards must first be highly desirable to the child and, secondly, must not be obtainable easily outside the conditions of the contract.

There are other important things to remember about setting up contracts. Always involve your child in making the initial agreement, even if it is a bit one-sided at that stage, and do not hesitate to re-state the contract periodically (perhaps every week or two) to keep it up to date. Agreements can usually be stated verbally; however, for more severe problems and with older children you may prefer to write things down, especially if the contract involves several things the child should be doing. This will reduce arguments later about whether or not the terms of the agreement were met. Besides these general suggestions there are some specific rules which should be closely followed in any agreements you make with your child:

Rule 1. If rewards are going to be used, the conditions of the contract should allow your child to achieve them at first without difficulty.

Rule 2. Any reward must come *after* the first conditions of the contract have been fulfilled, and *never* before. (With young children, there must be no delay between their completing their side of the bargain, and the parent's fulfilling his part.)

Rule 3. The contract must be honest, fair and clear. Leave no doubt as to what is expected of the child, and try to balance the amount of reward with this.

Rule 4. Be positive in your contract. Saying to your boy or girl 'when you finish your first course you can have your pudding' is more likely to result in his or her cooperation than 'if you don't eat your first course you can't have your pudding'.

Rule 5. Make sure you are able to be consistent and fulfil your side of the contract. Failure of a parent to keep his side of an agreement can lead to the sort of consequences shown in the following example:

Anthony was a twelve-year-old boy at secondary school. His behaviour had been difficult for a long time, even at junior school, and for the first two months of his second year he had been a constant problem for his teachers and other children; he often got into fights, was disruptive in class, and in general would never do what he was asked to do. One afternoon Anthony was made to stay behind at his desk when the others left. At this he lost his temper and threw everything out of his own and the surrounding desks. His parents were subsequently asked to come and see the headmaster to discuss what he was like at home and school and how they could all help him. Anthony's class-teacher was also at this meeting and suggested that they should try to set up some sort of contract between his parents, the teachers and Anthony, which would give him some incentive for giving up his aggressive and disruptive ways.

The scheme they worked out between them was one with which Anthony was in agreement and also pleased to try. His parents had said that they were thinking of buying a bicycle for Anthony, and it was decided that this would be their side of the contract. For his part Anthony would work towards this goal by being cooperative at school. The detailed plan entailed Anthony being awarded a point by his class teacher at the end of the day if there had been no reports in the school of his having been in a fight, or having been unduly aggressive or disruptive during the day. The teacher was to inform Anthony's parents regularly of how many points their son was gaining, so that they could also take part by showing their pleasure and interest in any progress he made. If Anthony had a fight or in other ways caused disruption at school, it was decided that he would lose five of the points he had earned. (A total of thirty points would be needed to get his bicycle.) The two sides of the bargain were written down in detail.

In the next few weeks Anthony did not become a model pupil, but at least he was much less hostile and aggressive to both staff and other children. In fact, after the first two weeks of settling down to the agreement, he did not behave badly at school for over a month, and was therefore well on his way to earning his thirty points. Unfortunately, at this stage his parents, in the hope of making sure the good behaviour would go on longer, said they would give the bike at his birthday, which was another six weeks off. The result was not unexpected. Anthony's behaviour became worse at home and at school. He was rude and defiant to his parents and teachers, truanted, hit two younger boys and generally caused great disturbance for several days, so that he was suspended from school for the remainder of the term.

It is clear that Anthony's parents broke the contract and his reaction, though exaggerated, was predictable in the circumstances. It also means that future attempts by his parents to control his unruly behaviour are likely to be more difficult because he has learnt that at least on this occasion they were not to be trusted.

Discussion of 'What do you do?' (p. 85)

1. When trying to increase the interest of a child in school-work, or anything else, it is essential that you reward for trying as well as for successes. In this example all four answers are rewards for the child. However, although each of these reinforcement procedures is satisfactory, using them in combination (D) would probably be the most efficient method.

Giving praise to a child is of course of primary importance. Giving some small prize would also work well for many children. Teaching a child that stars will later be exchanged for a small prize is a good way of helping her to see the progress she is making. Place the chart in a prominent place, but fill it in yourself at the beginning at least; draw a picture of the prize at the end of the series of stars. Here is an example of what a chart could look like:

This child has earned two stars towards her prize.

2. When you set up a contract with your child, whether it is by word of mouth or written down, you should keep in mind the rules mentioned in this chapter.

In answer (A) it is not stated what Patrick would have to do to be 'helpful'. So what would he do to earn the surprise? Answer (B) is wrong because it is a negative contract, threatening to take away a reward if he does not work on his room. Answer (C) is the best contract because it defines

93

what the child should do and what the reward is. By checking the room Mother will be able to decide whether the child can watch the television or not. Answer (D) is clearly a threat of punishment and therefore not a successful procedure.

3. In this example the child is trying to make a contract. If the parents agree to either (A) or (B) they will not have made a good contract. In agreement (A) the reinforcement comes before the child's performance of the task, while in agreement (B) the reward is out of keeping in both type and amount for the task carried out. Try to balance the child's side of the contract with your own – this example is hardly a contract, but a child arranging his own reward for eating something! For answers (C) and (D) both the task and consequences appear fair and clear.

Follow-up quiz

Point out what is wrong with each of the following four contracts, choosing from this list of faults.

- A. Dishonest
- B Unfair
- C Reward given before performance
- D Not clear
- E Inconsistent
- F Reward delayed
- G Negative contract

1. 'All right John, you can go out and play this morning, but you must do your weekend homework this afternoon.'

Mistake: ....

2. 'Alison, if you clear all the weeds out of the garden, I will give you 5p.' [It would take her two hours].

Mistake: ....

3. 'David, if you will empty the rubbish-bins each week this spring, I will take you horse-riding in the summer.'

Mistake: ....

4. 'Be a good girl at dinner, Mandy, and then you won't miss your pudding.'

Mistake: ....

9. Putting together a programme

What do you do?

Steven is a twelve-year-old boy living with his mother and
older brother. His mother is a good cook and he loves food.
His main problem as far as his mother is concerned is that
he will not come in on time for a meal in the evening; but
she always makes something for him however late he is.

1. If you were advising his mother what to do, which of the
   following actions would you recommend her to take first
   of all?
   A Tell Steven he can have supper only if he is in by a
     certain time.
   B Decide the precise time by which he must come home.
   C Record his present behaviour before attempting to
     change it.

2. Two of the following are the most important steps for
   Steven's mother to take and can be carried out simul-
   taneously:
   A Note what time he comes in in the evenings.
   B Think of things he likes or wants which will encourage
     him to come in earlier.
   C Scold him or punish him if he comes in later.

3. When she is trying to change his habit, how should
   Steven's mother make sure she is being effective?

A By her record and graphs of what is happening.
B By her impression that she is not having to wait for him so often.
C By friends or neighbours commenting on Steven's improvement.

The purpose of this chapter is to show how the techniques described in earlier chapters can be combined to make a plan of campaign to deal with a problem. Let's remind ourselves of the basic points again, before doing this.

The importance of observing accurately and describing clearly what your children are actually doing has been stressed. It may still be difficult to think in such terms, and to consider your own reactions carefully enough to release yourself from a subjective view of your own children which can be hampering when you are attempting to influence their behaviour. Despite this difficulty, if you go ahead and systematically define and record the actions of your children as described earlier, you will be in a better position to decide whether changes in the reactions of other people at home will be helpful for them. In a sense, you have now learned how to take the guesswork out of some of the things you have already been doing with your children. By following the recording procedure we have introduced you will see if and when changes are occurring in your children's behaviour, and you will know some of the reasons for these changes.

In the earlier chapters a good deal of emphasis was also put on the effect of encouraging or reinforcing some of the child's actions by doing something he finds rewarding immediately after them, like giving praise or other attention. You have to realize, of course, that this process works both ways. What your child does or says after you have behaved in a particular manner will also affect the way you act on future occasions. For instance, the problem of whether a child does not do as he is told because his mother is angry and hostile or whether his mother becomes angry with him because he is defiant is very much a chicken or egg question – it is difficult to know who is influencing whom most!

All children are different, both in their physical characteristics and in the setting in which they grow and develop. It is quite impossible to discuss all the things that might be

done in every situation and for every child. The only thing to do is to establish and present a general procedure by which parents can develop their own programmes to help their children. This chapter is therefore intended to draw together what might otherwise seem a group of unrelated techniques to show how they can be incorporated into a specific programme of help for an individual child.

A general outline

The sequence of steps to be followed whenever parents are

preparing to try to teach their children new or different ways of behaving can be set out in order:

1. Decide what it is about your child's behaviour that is causing him or others a problem. Define the specific activity in a manner that will enable you to observe and record what he does. (See Chapter 4.)

2. Make sure you are planning to record your child's activities, and not indirectly your own. (See Chapter 5.)

3. Start by making notes on and graphing his actions *before* you attempt to change them. Continue this until you are confident you have a picture of how those actions usually occur. (See Chapter 5.)

4. Note and list the things your child likes which could be used as rewards or ways of encouraging him later in the programme. (See Chapter 3.)

5. Observe precisely the conditions in which the activity you are concerned about occurs. (See Chapters 2 and 3.) The main factors are:
   i. What else was happening in the period leading up to it?
  ii. Where did it occur and who was there?
 iii. What happened after the incident or action? For instance, did your child get ignored, was he given attention, did he get what he was after?

6. Decide on alternative activities which your child could do, and which you would want him to do, in place of the behaviour you are concerned about. These alternatives should also be ones which you would be able to reinforce with encouragement, praise, attention or rewards.

7. Choose the most appropriate technique to teach the new or alternative activity. (See Chapters 7 and 8.)

8. Make an outline for yourself of the programme you are going to use, with the following contents:
   i. Description of the behaviour problem.
  ii. The procedure you are going to use to teach the new or alternative activity.
 iii. The way you plan to reinforce the new or alternative activity.
  iv. The appropriate method of recording what happens.

9. Start your programme by using the suggested method for teaching the new or alternative activity, and by quite deliberately arranging the consequences of your child's actions.

10. Record samples of the activity regularly throughout the programme.

11. If the programme is altering your child's behaviour as shown in your graphed records, then continue.

12. If the progress is poor or variable, check:
   i. Whether you are reinforcing the new activity as recommended (see Chapters 2 and 3) or are still paying more attention to the old habits.
  ii. Whether the reinforcement used is sufficiently powerful – does the child find it encouraging enough to make him change?
 iii. Whether you have chosen an appropriate alternative activity.

Previous chapters have given you some idea of the techniques you will need, and now you know the overall plan of any programme of action as presented in the present chapter. You can practise this general programme first of all by choosing one of your child's minor problems and attempting to alter his way of doing things by systematically going through the sequence of steps.

Discussion of 'What do you do?' (p. 96)

It is very likely that Steven, the boy in this example, would come in for supper on time if his mother did not make any special provision for him when he was late. Food for Steven is enjoyable and rewarding, and his mother is in a sense encouraging him to stay out late by providing food later especially for him. In these circumstances many parents forget the necessary initial step of deciding and making clear to the child just what getting in on time means (Answer 1: B). Once this has been done, the mother or older brother can begin to note how late Steven is each evening, while at the same time thinking of things he would like or want which could later be used to reward any improvement (Answer 2: A and B).

After the preliminary information has been collected, a programme for changing the boy's habit is started. Although Steven's mother may feel happy about the results she should mainly judge the success of the procedures by the information gathered on his behaviour in the evenings (Answer 3: A).

Follow-up quiz

Rearrange the following six steps in the correct order for establishing a programme to teach new habits to your child.

.... A Check your recorded information to see whether your programme is working.

.... B Work out a method of observing and recording.

.... C Define what it is your child is doing that you want to change.

101

.... D Alter the programme if it is not being
effective.

.... E Outline a programme which includes
the teaching method, the rewards to be
used and the recording procedure.

.... F Collect information on what your child
is doing before you make any changes.

10. Cooperation at home and at school

What do you do?

Write an outline of the steps the parents should take to help
their children in the following examples:
1. Anthony is a bright, adventurous boy of nine, self-
confident and fearless. He is very popular with all the local
boys and liked by his teacher at school, who encourages him
in his favourite hobby of collecting stamps. At home there
are three younger children.

There have been various family crises and stresses in the
last year, and because of this the parents' behaviour towards
the children has been inconsistent for a while. Sometimes
they have been irritable, shouting at the children for making
a noise which they would not normally bother about. At
other times they have just ignored aggressive and destructive
behaviour in the children because they were preoccupied
with their own worries. This period has fortunately come to
an end, so that both parents are now relaxed and able to
spend time with the children again. Unfortunately, Anthony's
behaviour, which became difficult during the family problems, has not reverted to what it was before. Anthony had
previously been reasonably cooperative at home, but since
the one-year crisis period he has begun to stay out late, does
not help in the house, and generally does not do anything
his mother asks him to do. His father sometimes punishes
him for this, while on other occasions there is an argument

Children and parents

between the parents about what they should do instead. Even the occasional physical punishment from his father does not have any lasting effect, and in fact Anthony has tended to become more troublesome rather than less. When he has been most difficult his parents have sent him on weekends to stay with his aunt in the country. Whenever he is with her he behaves well, and she is pleased to have him. Anthony's parents want to know what to do.

2. Up to two years ago Gill had been doing very well at school, but now at the age of fourteen her teachers are getting worried about the decline in the standard of her work and have said so to her parents when they went for an interview at the school. Gill has always been an imaginative girl who will become engrossed in adventure stories in books and exciting films on television. Her parents have not had much education themselves and, although they are keen for their daughter to do well, they do not take a great deal of interest in her school work except to notice that she is not doing as much homework regularly as she used to.

Gill is in a class where the academic pressure is high, and the amount of homework has increased. The pattern of studying at home has been for Gill to do some work very thoroughly, then lose interest for a night or so and resort to a Western or horror film on television. After criticism from her teacher she will work well for another night or two, but then she loses interest again and slips back to watching television instead.

It is known that Gill is intelligent enough to cope with the work, and there are no reasons for her deteriorating achievement apart from a gradual loss of interest. Her parents and teachers are concerned about what they can do to help her along.

Answers: see Discussion of 'What do you do?' (p. 111).

Maintaining programmes at home

There are problems in being as thorough as we are advocating. First there is the problem of initial motivation – most people would rather not go to the trouble of trying anything which involves more effort than usual. Secondly, having started to use a programme parents often find it hard to go to the lengths of recording and graphing. A third difficulty

occurs in keeping a programme running once it has begun to show results. It is this last problem of maintaining the programme and keeping up your own interest and enthusiasm which we will deal with first.

In order to prevent the improvement usually shown after a little while on one of these programmes from fading gradually away, it is necessary to consider the suitability of the programme regularly. For example, the whole process quickly becomes stale and boring if the child continues to have some form of reinforcement only for completing simple maths problems which he has now mastered. Once the goal originally set has been achieved, new and perhaps more complex things should be set up as new goals. The recorded information, especially in graph form, is invaluable as an indicator of progress to show when the time has come for new procedures to be introduced in order to move up a step towards the next set goal. Your child will gradually begin to behave in ways which are closer to the end result you hoped for, as you systematically encourage some ways of behaving and discourage others.

Parents often forget to make sure that their own behaviour in carrying out the programmes and in persisting with them is adequately reinforced. The result may be that the parent stops trying and the programme fails. We are all dependent on some form of encouragement, and if it is not forthcoming the tendency is to give up, lose interest and avoid difficult situations rather than try to deal with them. It is, therefore, very important that you should think of ways of maintaining your own enthusiasm and willingness to persist with the scheme defore you start to put it into practice. But how? A most useful method is to get the cooperation of at least one other family member, so that you can keep each other going. Brothers and sisters can be trained to cooperate with parents in helping one another and maintaining each other's behaviour; husband and wife can support one another. For example, perhaps your husband or wife could reward you in some way for being consistent in your behaviour towards your child. Eventually you may work out contracts between yourself, the child and other family members, and recognize the need to build into the arrangement some reinforcement for yourself to help you keep going.

The very act of collecting information about what your

child does makes you aware of your own actions at the same time, and also keeps up your interest for a while. But making systematic observations and records every day can be very difficult to keep up. Once you have observed and recorded thoroughly before beginning to try to make changes, and have thus gained some experience, you can take some short-cuts. For instance, you can delay making further records for several days or even weeks until you have given your new method of encouragement a chance to have some effect. Then you only need make spot checks at intervals of a few days, or you can note what is happening only at certain times of day for a limited period two or three times a week. The important thing to remember, whatever shortened method you use, is that the time and the circum-stances of the observations should be kept the same through-out the period of recording.

Coordination between home and school

Some children are nervous or difficult both at home and at school, others only in one place or the other. Family relation-ships do not always prepare children for the sorts of relation-ships they will experience later with teachers and other children; this is sometimes the basis of difficulties at school. Parents and teachers can, however, work together to help children enjoy school and work at their own level of ability. To do this means using similar methods of encouragement or reinforcement in both settings – inconsistency between home and school may lead to problems in one or the other situation. For example, children who at home are used to being physically punished and restricted for misdemeanours, rather than having their good behaviour encouraged by interest and appreciation, may tend to get out of hand in primary school where there are less or different constraints. At the other extreme, children who have never had to try and control their impulses, learn to share, and tolerate frustration to some degree, are likely to find adaptation to school very difficult. The most important thing is for teacher and parents to get to know each other's views of the situation, so that they can work together. This means using similar rewards or other reinforcements in the same way in the different settings.

One way of doing this is to encourage activities in one situation by providing some form of reward in the other setting. For example, a teacher may give points, stars or some other token for making an effort at school in work or general behaviour; the parents can then exchange the tokens at home for something they know their child would like. Similarly encouragement at home to work on part of the preparation for a school project might be reinforced by the teacher's appreciative interest.

You must remember that you will influence your child's attitudes to school and work in the same way that you encourage or discourage anything else he does. The same principles hold true in all situations. Some parents find it difficult to be interested in what their children do at school, others spoil their interest by being too anxious about it. In either case the parents' attitude can be one of the contributing factors if a child is having unexpected difficulties at school with work or in his general behaviour, or begins to be reluctant to go to school at all.

In order to spot minor difficulties before they become established problems you need to keep up to date about your child's progress and behaviour at school. Teachers can often give you an idea of your child's social development as well as his academic progress. By visiting the school and discussing any difficulties the child is having there or at home most problems can be understood, and parents and teacher can often work out a way of helping the child together, using some of the general ideas suggested in this book.

Working and playing together

Besides learning how to deal with problems once they have arisen, what can we do to prevent them developing, and to provide a happy environment for the whole family? Whatever each individual's way of behaving, it has been learned; we learn to shout, steal, lie, be kind, be loving. People living together in a family also learn to function as members of that group. This learning starts in the first weeks after birth and continues throughout life. In this important process the parents are the teachers by example and by instruction.

In thinking about bringing up children, parents often have definite but conflicting ideas or are unsure of themselves; they cannot always rely on experiences in their own childhood to work out their own behaviour as parents. There are, however, some things that everyone can do and provide, taking cues from observing what children do when given the opportunity to behave spontaneously.

First you need to make sure that a child has the opportunity to play in a variety of ways of his own choosing. This means having a range of simple toys and materials with which to do and make things. Money is not important – a train made (by the child and parent) from cans and buttons and painted at home can be every bit as satisfying as a toy costing fifty times as much. It is very important also that parents should be involved in and encourage children's play. This cannot be emphasized too much. It is saddening to hear comments like 'I haven't time just now', or 'Don't bother me', or 'Go and ask your brother'. He may not want his brother, he probably wants you. You do not always have to be thinking in terms of 'what shall we play' or 'what shall I suggest he plays with'? Children learn from doing things *together with* an adult. Not only that – they enjoy it. In general we tend to underestimate children's understanding and capability, so that we over-protect them and fail to let them use the talents they have. By encouraging children to get involved in family affairs and to participate in the running of the home at a young age, and then expressing appreciation of their help, we teach them that things are more enjoyable at home when they join in. They also learn that home life involves some jobs which are just not fun, but still have to be done.

To achieve this kind of interaction the family has to be all together on occasions. With so many demands on each person's time it is sometimes necessary to arrange a regular family activity time – perhaps once a week, or more frequently if you can. Some parents set aside one evening for the family to be together. The children should be involved in deciding what to do and who should do what, and it is up to each person to plan his week so that he can be there. This evening should not be a grumble session, but rather an enjoyable time when, in twos, threes or all together, everyone can participate. The possibilities for activities are endless – sports, games, music, story or play reading, eating together, talking, sharing of hobbies. The important thing is that the family should learn to do things together, forming a basis for the children to participate eventually with others outside the family. Watching other people involved in sports, drama, and so on, is valuable experience and fun too, but a child also needs to learn how to take part, and how to develop and show his special talents.

Besides learning these social skills first at home, children also learn about love, affection, helping, providing, sharing, communicating and all other aspects of human interaction chiefly from other family members. To a great extent a child learns to be an individual in his home, and what sort of person he develops into is largely a result of the practices of his parents. Children learn about being an adult from the example which their parents provide, and this of course includes how parents behave towards one another.

Don't let your child down. Care enough to observe him, get to know him, set up some rules and limits for him, provide him with examples of how you would like him to behave, and teach him. For some problems, care enough to record and graph and then change things. Be consistent, and show your love frequently with understanding, encouragement and praise.

Solutions and discussion of 'What do you do?' (p. 103)

1. Programme outline for Anthony

a. Definition of problem. Define exactly what Anthony does that distresses his parents: i. *staying out late* – precisely, 'coming in after 9 p.m. on five nights a week'; ii. *untidiness* – 'leaving his clothes on the floor and not putting his toys away'; iii. *disobedience* – 'not doing anything he is asked or told to do unless it is repeated forcefully or with a threat'.

b. Teaching procedure. Give him some form of token reward for doing what he is asked to do, being helpful and co-operative, clearing away his toys and clothes, coming in on time.

c. Reinforcement to be used. Exchange tokens for i. stamps for his collection; ii. extra visits to his aunt. (It would also be wise to look into what he finds satisfying at his aunt's that he no longer gets from home.)

d. Recording method. i. Specify what you expect Anthony to do around the house and note the number of times he does and does not do as you ask. Record the numbers for the whole day. ii. Record whether he comes in on time or not.

e. Programme for parents. Share the responsibility for recording if possible. Note for each other how often each parent rewards, punishes or ignores Anthony's behaviour and reward one another in some way (if only by support and encouragement) when Anthony's behaviour is responded to appropriately.

2. Programme outline for Gill

a. Definition of problem. Define what Gill does that interferes with her learning: i. watching television when she should be doing homework; ii. being inconsistent in her study time, using cramming sessions to try and make up for times when she did no work at all.

b. Teaching procedure. i. Find out what homework needs to be done each evening. ii. Make television viewing dependent on a certain amount of homework being completed. iii. Set up a reward system at home for marks earned in school for the homework.

c. Reinforcement to be used. Give i. One hour of television following an hour of study; ii. Interest, encouragement and praise for having made a good effort at homework, as reported by her teachers, with other small rewards if merited; iii. Extra or increased pocket money or other suitable reward for a good report from her teachers at the end of term (not necessarily based on marks gained, but more on work done).

d. Recording method. i. Record what proportion of the assigned work she gets done. ii. Record how much time she spends on her homework. iii. Record the marks or grades earned at school for homework.

e. Teacher–parent cooperation. To carry out this programme parents will have at least to find out from teachers what Gill is expected to do for homework, and to receive from the teachers an estimate of the quality of the homework done in the form of marks, etc. Even closer cooperation, with teachers and parents planning the programme together, would obviously make it more likely to be successful.

Follow-up

The time has come to put the ideas into practice. From now on the real follow-up will be what you actually do with your own children.

The techniques described in this book are to some extent a part of all successful parents' ways of caring for their children. The parents of happy and socially well-adjusted children are seen to be consistent and rewarding in their relationships with the children. But we all have some things we would like to help our children with; perhaps you have already tried without success, or have been wondering what to do. You have read what seems to help others, and there are some sample programmes in Appendix 1, starting on the next page. Why not get started now?

113

Appendix 1. Sample programmes to help you start

To show how the principles we have outlined are used, here are programmes for dealing with some common behaviour problems. The programmes were used at a children's therapy unit, and have been found to be successful by many families. The areas dealt with are as follows:

I. Children who are so untidy that they cannot find anything in their rooms.

II. Children who avoid doing or refuse to do their share of household chores.

III. Children who need help to study at home regularly.

I. Teaching children to pick up things in their rooms

These programmes are for parents who have trouble with their children leaving things scattered all over the place. Three alternative programmes are presented, and it is up to parents to decide which one would benefit their child.

Programme A

This programme is for younger children who leave toys around their rooms, or for older children who leave clothes, toys or other things they have used lying around. The programme assumes that the child enjoys the use of the objects concerned. If this is not so, the programme will be ineffective and another should be chosen. The main procedure consists of the parents removing for a period of time anything left out of place. The method of doing this is as follows:

1. Decide on a specific time each day when you will check the room. The child may be present or absent at that time, but most parents find that the best time is just after the child has gone to school.

2. Prepare a place such as a cupboard or trunk which can be locked, in which all things left around will be placed.

3. Decide how long the items removed will be placed 'in storage'. The main idea is to place things in storage long enough for the child to miss them. If a child with an extensive wardrobe leaves things around, you may want to place them in storage for a week or ten days before returning them. For a child with a very limited wardrobe, a day or two might be sufficient.

4. Tell the child that items which are not in their correct place will be put in storage for the specified time. Make sure that there is no question as to where the 'correct place' is. If you mean only that they should *not* be on the bed or on the floor, let your child know this.

   Also tell the child that each evening you will return the things due to come out of storage and put them on the floor of the child's room. Tell him that they will go back in storage if they are not in their places when you check the next morning.

5. Each time you put items into storage mark on each one when it should be brought back into circulation again, and each evening make sure you return items due back.

6. Do not argue about or discuss the programme, other than explaining how it operates.

Programme B

This programme is for older children. It should be used only under these specific circumstances: the child leaves things around, and the parent has picked them up and put them away in the past. To use this programme it is assumed that the child will find an extremely cluttered room unpleasant. The programme will not work with a child for whom this is not true.

The method is simple. Leave everything in the child's room, without picking up or tidying anything. If clothes are left out, leave them as they are. Make no comments on the messy room, and do not request the child to clean up. If the room gets to be an eyesore, shut the door.

The programme assumes that the child has left things around because the parent has been cleaning up for him and, disliking a messy room, will now begin to clear it up himself. If after a reasonable trial (such as two weeks) the programme does not work, try one of the others.

Programme C

This programme is for a younger child, or for an older child for whom it appears unlikely that either Programme A or B would work. The basic idea is to check the room at a set time each day, as in Programme A, and to give the child a point-score between 0 and 3 depending upon the condition of his room. These points are then used to earn some privilege.

1. Decide upon a time each day when you will check the room. The child may or may not be present.
2. Give the child points for the condition of his room. A score of 3 means the room is tidy, an above average performance; a score of 2 means the room has just a few things around, and can be considered a typical satisfactory performance. A score of 1 means the room was pretty messy, and a zero indicates chaos.
3. Put up a chart in the child's room. This should show how many points the child gets each day. Each time you inspect, mark the score on the chart.
4. Decide on some privilege which the child can earn with the points. It may be something the child already receives, such as being allowed to watch TV, or receiving all his pocket money. Make each point worth a certain amount of the privilege.

   If the privilege is to be something the child does not already receive regularly, at the beginning select something small enough to be used for frequent rewards. Whatever you use, decide on a specific number of points required for a certain amount of privilege. You may also put on the chart or in the room some indication of the value of the points.

5. Depending on the privilege to be earned, the points may be traded in daily or once a week. The more frequently the better, especially with younger children. It is also quite acceptable to allow the child to trade points in whenever he wishes to and has enough to trade. At the trade-in time add up the points the child has to date, let him trade as many as he wants, and mark the number left on the chart. Points left at the end of a week can be saved for the future; just mark the number of points saved from the previous week or weeks on the new sheets of the chart.

6. Before starting the programme, describe it to the child. Be quite clear in indicating what behaviour will obtain points, and how many points will be earned for different degrees of room tidiness. Explain the trade-in procedure and the privileges which can be earned by points. Make clear that he cannot receive these privileges in any other way. Show him the chart and how it will be filled in. Do not argue, or debate the programme. Describe it, and indicate that you will leave it to him whether or not he wants to clear his room to earn points and privileges. Then do exactly that – leave it to the child.

7. Remember to be consistent when you have decided on a system.

II. Cutting down dawdling

'Dawdling' is a rather vague term which is used here to describe the sort of behaviour that occurs when a child is asked to do something, or has some specific task he is expected to do regularly at a particular time, and he either does not do the task in a reasonable length of time, or does other things instead, such as playing with something, looking at a book or magazine, talking, mild complaining, 'restless' wandering about, and so forth.

Examples of dawdling might be slowness in dressing or undressing, in getting outer clothes on or off, in setting the table, in taking out the rubbish, in coming in to dinner when called, and so on.

The programme will *not* cover situations where there is any question about the child's ability to perform the task. It is assumed that on previous occasions he has done it, so it is known that he is able to do what is required. The programme also does *not* cover the situation where the child occasionally does not do what he is asked because it interrupts some activity in which he is involved (and that sometmes includes imaginative 'dreaming' as well as practical play).

The procedure is based upon the assumption that children dawdle for one or more of the following reasons:

1. Dawdling results in a lot of attention from adults.
2. They avoid having to do something unpleasant by dawdling.
3. There are no different consequences for doing the job promptly as against doing it slowly.

The programme attempts to do the following:

1. Remove the attention-getting value of dawdling.
2. Not reward dawdling by letting the child avoid the chore.
3. Arrange 'naturally' occurring pleasant consequences for getting something done, compared with less pleasant consequences for dawdling.

The programme

1. If the child is asked to do something, ask him once or

119

twice only. Ask him quite specifically and clearly; that is, do not say, 'please do your job', or 'haven't you something to do?' but say instead, 'please take out the rubbish' or 'please put your shoes on'. Do not make any threats or promises. Ask in a matter of fact way, as if you assume that he will comply. If he does not respond, ignore him, with no further comment or requests to do the job. Do *not* nag the child to do what you want; after asking him initially make no further comments concerning his doing it or not doing it, except as described in the following sections.

2. Where it is possible, do not let him avoid the task by dawdling. If he does not do as you ask, do not do his job for him unless it is absolutely necessary. If a child does not set the table for dinner, you might have to do it for him in some circumstances; but if he does not get dressed, let him be late until he does.

3. When he does perform the task in a reasonable amount of time, let him know you appreciate it. This need not be extreme, suggesting that the child has done something heroic and fantastic, but should be some indication of approval, praise or appreciation.

4. Try to arrange 'natural' unpleasant consequences for not performing on time. For example, he may be late for school or miss some activity or outing if he does not dress and get ready in time. If a child does not come when called, especially for something such as meals or activities that he enjoys, start without him or let him miss some of it.

5. Be patient. When he is slow, do not rush to do the job for him. If possible do not let him go on to another activity without completing the task. Often you can arrange things to make this easier to programme. For instance, if one of your children is to take out the rubbish,

ask him to do it five minutes before a television programme he wants to watch. If he has not done it by then,
tell him in a matter-of-fact way that when the rubbish is
emptied he can watch the programme. If he misses the
beginning, he misses the beginning.

6. Try to arrange it so that 'good' things follow doing the
task over which the child usually dawdles, as in the above
example in which television was arranged to follow the
rubbish-emptying.

7. Work on only one thing at a time. If your child dawdles
when dressing, eating, and in six other situations, try to
work on dawdling in *one* situation only; when you have
reasonable improvement start on a second, rather than
attacking on eight fronts at once.

8. Write down your programme, specifying what behaviour
you are working on, when and where he is to do it, how
you will ask him, what will happen if he does do it
reasonably, and what will happen if he does not. Make
sure all adults or older children are aware of the programme, to ensure that everyone involved will be
consistent.

III. Helping your child learn to do homework

'Doing homework' refers to a number of things. Three
aspects of doing homework are:

1. Working steadily and regularly for a reasonable length of
time.

2. Using effective studying methods for whatever amount of
time is spent on homework.

3. Showing later that the material covered has been learned
and retained.

Obviously, these three aspects are related. This programme covers only the first aspect of doing homework – learning to spend time regularly on homework. It is specifically designed for an older pupil for whom getting down to doing homework has already become a problem, or for a young child who is just beginning to have homework assignments, although some of the ideas are applicable to an older student who is already persisting relatively well.

Study setting

A study space in which the child will do his homework should meet the following requirements as far as possible:

1. It should have the physical necessities, such as adequate light, a satisfactory place to write, comfortable but businesslike chair, and so forth. Supplies such as pencils, pencil sharpener, glue, erasers, rulers and such should be available without leaving the study area.
2. The study area should ideally be in a place where the child does not usually do anything except study. The dining-table, play area, or places where the child listens to records, entertains friends, talks on the telephone, watches TV, eats, builds models or does anything except studying are not ideal. Whenever the child studies at home he should be in the study area; whenever he is not studying, even for a three-minute break, he should not be in the study area.
3. The study area need not be a separate room, although this is best. It should be arranged so that when in the study area the child is screened from the sight and sound of other people or activities. If the study area is not a separate room, it should be arranged so that he does not face the rest of the room.
4. There should be no telephones, TV sets, record-players,

food, pictures, books, magazines or other distractions unrelated to the current homework assignment in the study area.

Time spent on homework

The child is said to have done his homework if he works for a length of time called the 'homework period'. For a young child who has never had homework to do before, the length of the homework period should initially be ten minutes. For an older child who rarely does his homework at all, the initial length should also be ten minutes. For an older child who sometimes spends time on homework and sometimes does not, the initial length of the homework period should be the average time he spends doing homework over five days. If this average time is less than ten minutes, start with a ten-minute initial period.

Before starting the programme the child and his parents should decide upon the time at which he will start doing his homework. If possible this should be at about the same time on each day that homework is to be done.

Whether or not the child does his homework is optional. The parents should never instruct him to do his homework, reprimand him if he does not, cajole him, urge him, threaten him, or do anything else to get him to work. The way to improve his own motivation will be described later.

Assessing success in doing homework

Each day the child's behaviour during the study period is given a score. There are three scores, which are:

1. *Success.* This means that the child worked for the entire homework period. No attention is paid to whether he completed his assignments or did his homework correctly. If he spent the required amount of time in the study area

and you did not definitely see him doing other things instead, the child's word is the basis for judging whether or not he worked.

2. *Failure*. This means that the child went to the study area, but did not work for the entire homework period.

3. *No game*. This means that the child did not go to the study area. This may be because he had no homework. It may be because he did his homework elsewhere. It may be because he did not do his homework at all. In all cases this is scored 'no game'.

Changing the length of the homework period

If the child gets five success ratings with no failure between the first and last, increase the length of the homework period by five minutes. Ignore all 'no game' days. Keep doing this until the homework period reaches a duration his teachers consider adequate for his age and school class. If you have doubts about the amount or type of homework, or even if it should be done at all, consult the teacher, not the child.

If he wishes to finish something after the homework period has expired, he may, but *not* in the study area. Work done outside this area is not considered homework for the purposes of this programme.

Providing motivation for 'success'

With a young child, a special but small privilege or treat should be given for 'success'. At the start of each week this should be decided on in discussion with him. It may be the privilege of staying up fifteen minutes longer on 'success' days. It may be a special trip for five or more 'successes'. It may be some other privilege. The parent and the child are the best judges of what is appropriate.

For an older child who has difficulty in working, a slightly different approach is usually more successful. Select as a reward something he would very much like to do or have. You will know what this is. Typical rewards used by parents are watching TV, listening to a record-player, going out with friends at night, additional pocket money, and so forth.

The greatest problem is determining how much of the privilege is earned by each day of 'success' in doing homework. The guiding rule is as follows: each success should be worth enough for the child to receive *more* of the privilege if he succeeds every day than he now does; but each success should have a low enough value for the child to receive *less* of the privilege than he does now if he shows no improvement.

Here is an illustration. One boy whose programme started with a ten-minute homework period liked to watch TV all the time. His parents estimated that in recent weeks they had allowed him to watch TV for about an hour a day. They also estimated that in recent weeks he had done at least ten minutes of homework about one third of the time, that is, one day in three. If they made each success worth ninety minutes of TV, he would have to be successful about two thirds of the time to watch as much TV as he did before the study programme started – that is, one hour a day. However, if he always did his homework he would be allowed to watch ninety minutes a day, that is, half as much again as before the study programme started.

The parents worked out these values by estimating how much TV they now allowed him to watch and how much each success need be worth if he were to get half as much again for being 'perfect' in completing homework periods. Of course, the value of a success does not change as the length of the homework period increases. In this case, each success would remain worth ninety minutes of TV, even when success meant completing an hour-long homework period.

Let the child spend his rewards as he wants; that is, allow him to save them up for the future or to spend them daily.

Do not give any reward if he does not score a success. Similar calculations will allow you to decide on the value of a success if you use other rewards. Do not use anything as a reward unless you are willing to let him have even more of it than he is currently getting when he starts succeeding regularly. The value of each success should be such that if the child does his homework every day, he will get more of the reward than he did before.

Encourage the older pupil to suggest possible ways of keeping up his own interest and motivation to work, and to let you know if he would prefer to change to a different system. If one reward seems to lose its appeal, change to a different one. However, do not change if the pupil does not wish to do so, as long as he is regularly scoring successes.

With young children, when you first start the programme it is best to have a privilege or treat which they can earn daily. This is also best for older children at the very beginning of the programme. If you feel up to it, you can allow them to trade in successes for a variety of rewards.

Keeping a record of studying habits

On the wall or desk in the study area, put the following:

1. A table showing how much each success is worth.
2. A notice stating the current length of the study period.
3. A chart showing how many successes (if any) the child has saved up towards privileges. This should be corrected daily.

Discussion with the child

Before starting the programme explain all of it to the child and discuss it with him. If at any time he has questions about the operation of the programme, clarify it for him.

You must be very matter-of-fact about homework. It

may take a while before you notice any effects. Other than setting up the programme (with or without his help), you leave all responsibility to the child. Do not try and force him in any way to do homework. Once discussed and settled, avoid any argument with him over the programme. If he does not like the rules or regulations, just remind him in a matter-of-fact way that this is what you both agreed on for the time being. If he continues to argue, tell him you have things to do and *leave*. Do this consistently.

There is one exception to the statement above. Successes should be praised and long-term improvement appreciated. However, ignore failures or 'no games'.

Check-list of steps for all programmes

Wherever you are trying to help a child, at school or at home, the general way to set about it is always much the same. Here is a check-list to go through to make sure you have remembered everything.

1. Have I defined clearly the behaviour I want to change?
2. Have I decided when the observations are to be made?
3. Have I thought how the information is to be collected?
4. Have I recorded the child's usual behaviour before I attempt to change it?
5. Is the information accurate?
6. Have I made graphs of the information?
7. Have I recorded the behaviour before change long enough to show how regular or irregular it is?
8. Has a programme for changing his behaviour been written out?
9. Am I able to control what happens when he behaves in his usual way?

10. Have I got sufficient ways of rewarding or reinforcing the sort of behaviour I want him to achieve?
11. Do I use reinforcement dependent on what he does, rather than when I feel like it?
12. Have I made it possible to follow all the procedures of the programme?
13. Can I follow them *consistently*?
14. Have I made sure that I get some encouragement for persisting with the observing and recording, and for responding appropriately?

Appendix 2. Recording-sheets

Sample sheet for recording how often a child behaves in a stated way (p. 43)

Week of ....Name ....

Actions to be observed:

1.

2.

3.

Date .... Monday   Comments:

                   1. ....

                   2. ....

                   3. ....

Date .... Tuesday   Comments:

                   1. ....

                   2. ....

                   3. ....

Appendix 2

Date .... Wednesday   Comments:

           1. ....

           2. ....

           3. ....

Date .... Thursday   Comments:

           1. ....

           2. ....

           3. ....

Date .... Friday   Comments:

           1. ....

           2. ....

           3. ....

Date .... Saturday   Comments:

           1. ....

           2. ....

           3. ....

Date .... Sunday   Comments:

           1. ....

           2. ....

           3. ....

General Comments:

Sample sheet for recording child's responses to instructions or requests to behave in stated ways (p. 48)

Instructions:	Key:
1.	+ Did it correctly.
2.	/ Tried, but only got it partially correct.
3.	− Responded, but not correctly.
4.	0 Didn't try.
5.	
6.	
7.	
8.	
9.	
10.	

Name ....

Appendix 2

Sample sheet for recording whether a particular action occurs in a stated interval (pp. 51–2)

Name .... Date ....

Length of interval ....
(e.g. 1 minute, 5 minutes, etc.)

Interval	1	2	3	4	5	6	7	8	9	10	11	12	13	14	15
Actions 1															
2															
3															

Interval	16	17	18	19	20	21	22	23	24	25	26	27	28	29	30
Actions 1															
2															
3															

Interval	31	32	33	34	35	36	37	38	39	40	41	42	43	44	45
Actions 1															
2															
3															

Totals:

Action 1. ....

Action 2. ....

Action 3. ....

Sample sheet for a graph of the child's progress (pp. 59–61)

Name ....Programme...........................

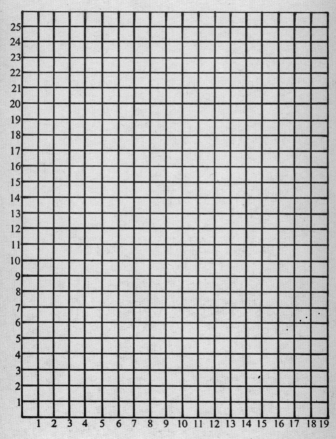

Number of times

Time period (usually days)

More about Penguins and Pelicans

Penguinews, which appears every month, contains details of all the new books issued by Penguins as they are published. From time to time it is supplemented by *Penguins in Print*, which is a complete list of all titles available. (There are some five thousand of these.)

A specimen copy of *Penguinews* will be sent to you free on request. For a year's issues (including the complete lists) please send 50p if you live in the British Isles, or 75p if you live elsewhere. Just write to Dept EP, Penguin Books Ltd, Harmondsworth, Middlesex, enclosing a cheque or postal order, and your name will be added to the mailing list.

In the U.S.A.: For a complete list of books available from Penguin in the United States write to Dept CS, Penguin Books Inc., 7110 Ambassador Road, Baltimore, Maryland 21207.

In Canada: For a complete list of books available from Penguin in Canada write to Penguin Books Canada Ltd, 41 Steelcase Road West, Markham, Ontario.

The Normal Child

And Some of His Abnormalities

C. W. Valentine

In recent years a great deal of nonsense has been written and spoken about 'Child Psychology'. In particular many things have been wrongly regarded as signs of abnormalities by persons whose studies have been confined largely to problem children, and whose knowledge of normal children is very limited.

This book, by one of the leading authorities on the psychology of childhood, gives a clear introduction to the study of child psychology, stressing the great range of individual differences among mentally healthy children of normal intelligence. The account of the early years is freely illustrated by observations and experiments made almost daily by the author on his own five children and by the records and researches of many other well-qualified psychologists.

No previous knowledge of psychology is assumed.

Child Care and the Growth of Love

John Bowlby

In 1951, under the auspices of the World Health Organization, Dr John Bowlby wrote a report on *Maternal Care and Mental Health* which collated expert world opinion on the subject and the issues arising from it – the prevention of juvenile and adult delinquency, the problem of the 'unwanted child', the training of women for motherhood, and the best ways of supplying the needs of children deprived of their natural mothers. This Pelican is a summary of Dr Bowlby's report, freed from many of its technicalities and prepared for the general reader.

This revised edition contains chapters based on an article by Dr Mary Salter Ainsworth, written in 1962 also for the World Health Organization when it once again made an important study of child care.

'It is a convenient and scholarly summary of evidence of the effects upon children of lack of personal attention, and it presents to administrators, social workers, teachers and doctors a reminder of the significance of the family' – *The Times*

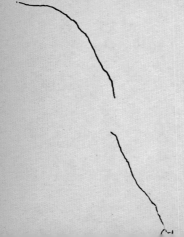

Children in Conflict

Morris Fraser

There are all too many children throughout the world who have known nothing but violence and fear, and for whom the threat of riot and war is a heavy and permanent shadow.

As a child psychiatrist in Belfast Dr Fraser combines intimate personal experience of Ulster with a first-class knowledge of world research on racial conflict. In this realistic and compassionate book he conveys the searing effect of violence on young minds, and suggests ways in which the reactions of children in situations of conflict can be understood and measures that can be taken to help them.

Ulster is only one area that produces its quota of damaged children, and there, as elsewhere, primary-school integration would contribute more than any other factor to peace. For, as the author warns us, while religious and racial segregation of schoolchildren exists, so too will community strife.

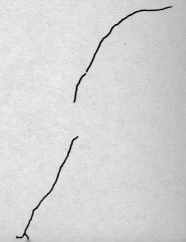

Children Under Stress

Sula Wolff

'This is an admirable book, which deserves to be widely read, not only by those who are professionally concerned with disturbed and unhappy children, but by that very large number of parents who are worried from time to time about their children's behaviour and who are uncertain about when to seek expert advice . . . It is the best summary known to me of what can be achieved by child psychiatry, and an excellent account of the causes and common manifestations of emotional disturbance in children' – Dr Anthony Storr

The Psychology of Childhood and Adolescence

C. I. Sandström

In this concise study of the processes of growing up Professor Sandström has produced a book which, although it is perfectly suited to the initial needs of university students and teachers in training, will appeal almost as much to parents and ordinary readers. His text covers the whole story of human physical and mental growth from conception to puberty.

Outlining the scope and history of developmental psychology, Professor Sandström goes on to detail the stages of growth in the womb, during the months after birth, and (year by year) up to the age of ten. There follow chapters on physical development, learning and perception, motivation, language and thought, intelligence, the emotions, social adjustment, and personality. The special conditions of puberty and of schooling are handled in the final chapters.

Throughout this masterly study the author necessarily refers to 'norms of development': these neatly represent the average stages of growing up, but (as Professor Mace comments in his introduction) they must only be applied to individual children with caution.